2020 VISION

2020 VISION

Today's business leaders on tomorrow's world

Tim Burt

First published 2015 by
Elliott and Thompson Limited
27 John Street
London WC1N 2BX
www.eandtbooks.com

ISBN: 978-1-78396-036-1

9 8 7 6 5 4 3 2 1

A CIP catalogue record for this book is available from the British Library.

Jacket design: Antigone Konstantinidou
Typeset by Marie Doherty
Printed in the UK by TJ International

CONTENTS

INTRODUCTION

In the second decade of the twenty-first century, there is a common refrain among the world's business leaders. From agriculture to mining, automobiles to telecommunications, industrialists say they have witnessed more upheaval in the past five years than at almost any other time since their companies were founded.

The pace of change has accelerated following the global financial crisis of 2008–09; the subsequent bank bailouts; a series of environmental and natural disasters; bloody and dangerous regional conflicts; regime change in North Africa; conflict in the Caucasus; and geo-political tensions from the western frontier of Russia to the eastern shores of China. Further rapid transformation is expected by 2020 as macro-economic events force companies to rethink their business models. This will have major implications for international trade, sourcing raw materials, manufacturing, employment, supply chains, regulations, pricing and consumption habits.

The corporate world of 2020 could look very different. Among global markets, the balance of power is likely to have shifted further to the high-growth economies of China and India, as well as the rising economic powers of Mexico, Indonesia, Nigeria and Turkey, among others. New technologies, digital communications, increasing environmental regulation, commodity shortages and decisions on fiscal and monetary policy will alter the way companies operate, potentially transforming their financial performance. Layered on to that, social and economic trends such as urban migration, changing social mobility and volatile consumer confidence could fundamentally alter the rules of supply and demand.

Companies are both nervous and optimistic about the uncertain road ahead. This book seeks to capture their anxieties and ambitions. In the following pages, business leaders from twenty different companies in twenty industries reveal their strategic objectives and market expectations for this era of change. Their views are relevant because each company is a leading indicator of economic activity, geographic expansion or changing consumer habits. Their business successes and failures reflect broader demand for goods and services. Their investment decisions symbolise the mood of the wider global economy. These activities – covered in this book – include advertising, aviation, automobiles, communications, consumer goods, education, energy, engineering, entertainment, food production, healthcare, institutional investing, legal services, marketing, media, mining, retailing, satellites, shipping and technology.

The cross-section is also geographic. Companies from Africa, Asia, Latin America, Russia and China are represented – along with those from the traditional business centres of Western Europe and North America. Those agreeing to take part include third-generation dynastic leaders of family-controlled companies, start-up entrepreneurs, women who broke through the corporate glass ceiling and people who joined large corporations on the factory floor and rose over decades to the top.

The wide-range of individuals and companies contributing to *2020 Vision* have one thing in common. They were all generous with their views and their time. It was an education to meet them.

In *2020 Vision*, some of the chairmen and chief executives are long-term acquaintances, dating back to when I was a correspondent at the *Financial Times* from the late 1980s into the new millennium. Others have been clients in my current role as a strategic communications adviser, frequently expressing anxiety and frustration about the sort of news reports that I once filed. Those anxieties have intensified partly due to the disposable nature of modern journalism, where stories now have a brief shelf life and investors are less interested in long-term vision than short-term returns. Their concerns also reflect the rise of shareholder activism, more aggressive regulation and the shortening life expectancy of chairmen and CEOs at publicly listed companies.

In the following twenty chapters, men and women from more than a dozen countries give candid assessments of the forces that will reshape their industries by the end of the decade. Together, the participant companies generate annual revenues of more than half a trillion dollars. Collectively, they directly employ more than 1.4 million people, and sustain the jobs of millions more in the wider supply chain. These companies also operate in almost every country in the industrialised world. Most of them are traded on stock markets; some are privately owned; others are partnerships. Many of the companies are large, mature players in their sectors. Others are newcomers, relative minnows on the corporate stage.

I would like to thank each chairman, chief executive, president and director for their time and patience. Our meetings took place in Brussels, Chicago, Cologne, Frankfurt, London, Los Angeles, Milan, New York, Oslo, Rome, Shanghai, Stockholm and Tokyo. We met in boardrooms and subsidiary offices, at overseas affiliates, in hotels and in the homes of those who have contributed.

They would not have participated at all were it not for the efforts and persuasive skills of Terri Behrik and Joel Parsons at BHP Billiton, Richard Smith at DMGT, Aldo Liguori at Fast Retailing, Lorna Montalvo at GE, Lars Witteck at Henkel, Emma Doherty at Houghton Mifflin Harcourt, Chris McLaughlin at Inmarsat, Beatrice Bondy at Investor, Christian Klick at Star Alliance, Charles Reynolds at Smith & Nephew, Will Tanous at Universal Music, Bobby Leach at VimpelCom, Chris Wade at WPP and Victor Young, Xiaolin Yuan and Ashley Sutcliffe at Zhejiang Geely. Countless others opened doors and checked facts, including Nick Coward, Alex Geiser, Anthony Silverman, Philip Gawith, Osvald Bjelland, Anthony Gordon Lennox, Richard Holloway, Julian Hanson-Smith, Ben Ullmann and Ian Limbach. They have been tolerant of questioning when it has been misinformed, and ready to correct basic errors. Any inaccuracies in the ensuing copy are mine alone.

My colleagues at StockWell, the London-based strategic communications firm, have been enormously supportive, as have all those at the publisher Elliott & Thompson. Olivia Bays, my editor, has been endlessly patient with numerous changes and delays. The entire enterprise would not have been possible without the hard work of my colleagues Alison Griffiths and particularly Juliet Snow, both of whom transcribed hours of conversations with accuracy and amazing good humour. Kate Heighes, Andrew Tosh and Nathan Minsberg at StockWell also helped with research. At the start of each chapter, I have compiled basic financial metrics and data on each company, accompanied by a short biography of the participating business leaders. The financial data is drawn from the 2013 and 2014 reported or forecast numbers for each company. The revenues have been translated from relevant local currencies into US dollars where necessary. At companies where profit margins have been impacted by significant accounting charges or non-operating items, I have relied on earnings before interest, tax, depreciation and amortisation. Any mistakes or factual errors are mine alone.

As with my last book, *Dark Art: The Changing Face of Public Relations*, my wife Helen has provided honest and tough advice. She has the best counsel on work–life balance that anyone could wish for. She says: 'Think twice before doing it again.'

Sir Martin Sorrell, WPP

Annual revenues: $16.7 billion
Operating profit margin: 15.1%
Number of employees: 179,000 including associates
Number of markets served: 111
Headquarters: London and New York

The British chief executive of the global advertising and marketing services group has been in the role since 1985. In that time WPP has grown to encompass a network of more than 3,000 offices, serving 342 of the Fortune Global 500 companies, every member of the Dow Jones 30 and sixty-eight companies in the NASDAQ 100. Sir Martin, knighted in 2000, is also a non-executive director of Alcoa, the US metals technology and engineering group, and Atlas Topco, the Formula 1 company. He is a board director of the Bloomberg Family Foundation; an advisory board director at Stanhope Capital and Bowmark Capital; and sits on the Executive Committee of the World Economic Forum International Business Council.

In the first season of *Mad Men*, mythical client-winner Don Draper tells an agency colleague: 'Advertising is based on one thing, happiness. And you know what happiness is? Happiness is the smell of a new car. It's freedom from fear. It's a billboard on the side of the road that screams reassurance that whatever you are doing is okay.'

Mad Men, of course, was set in an era when ad agencies were selling the American Dream. It was the age of Camelot with Kennedys in the White House – pre-Vietnam, pre-tobacco warnings, pre-recession. The Internet lay far beyond the horizon. In advertising, the laws of supply and demand were fairly predictable. Don Draper and his colleagues created reassuring marketing campaigns for household brands, and placed advertising on their behalf in newspapers and on TV, radio and billboards.

Fast-forward fifty years; the advertising world has been transformed. Data-gathering, behavioural profiling and programmatic bidding are threatening to eclipse the traditional crafts of Madison Avenue. Of the $1 trillion spent each year on global advertising and marketing communications, a growing proportion of ads are now distributed through computer algorithms and consumed on smartphones and tablets. Marketing campaigns are conceived with social networks in mind; audiences are tracked according to their data consumption habits; online exchanges can place ads automatically, driven by search-engine traffic.

At the centre of this industrial transformation sits Sir Martin Sorrell, the long-serving chief executive of WPP. He is the ringmaster of an advertising and marketing services group – spanning advertising, media and data investment, public relations and specialist communications – that comprises hundreds of companies, which, collectively, create and place one in four of all adverts around the world.

During almost thirty years as WPP chief executive, Sorrell has witnessed at first hand the upheaval in advertising and marketing caused – variously – by the onset of the digital age, accelerating globalisation, the emergence of China as an economic super-power, the fall of Soviet communism, several wars and financial crises that have come and gone. Over that time, the marketing group that emerged from the shell of UK manufacturer Wire and Plastic Products has grown rapidly as a result of both acquisition and organic expansion. By the second decade of the twenty-first century, WPP had evolved into a network of more than 3,000 offices employing almost 180,000 people in agencies and associate firms that represent two-thirds of the companies ranked in the Fortune Global 500.

A business at the heart of the creative industries – focused on developing advertising messaging and marketing power to sell all manner of products – is now evolving into a more mathematical, automated enterprise. Compelling ads still demand creative genius. But target audiences are identified increasingly using algorithms, data tracking and network technologies.

'Don Draper would hardly recognise much of what we do today,' says Sorrell. 'In future, there will be more "maths-men" and women than Mad Men in our industry, especially if the medium truly becomes more important than the message.

'We used to operate under a system where a campaign-planner would come up with the strategy; then we did the creative execution and from that we would distribute it. The creative department and the suits would then direct the media buyers. That is no longer always the case – even though traditional media and marketing disciplines are still critically important. Now we need more scientists, more engineers, more coding as we develop the business.'

Of WPP's annual revenues, digital marketing, media investment management and data investment management now account for $12 billion of the group's $16.7 billion total. As a proportion of total billings – the overall fees and commission-based income from clients – more than a third is derived from all forms of new media.

'The whole game is changing in two ways,' says Sorrell. 'Firstly, the skills we need are different. This is where the maths-men come in; we need people who are technologically literate; they are more often scientists compared with the arts pool we fished in before.

'Secondly, we have to integrate our services much more effectively. Clients are more confused because there are so many service options and the digital market is so fragmented. That creates an opportunity for

WPP because clients are turning to us more for advice, and seeking an integrated agency relationship around the world.'

This twin-track reorientation has emerged alongside four strategic priorities at WPP, which Sorrell hopes will enable the group to navigate the current market upheaval successfully and continue expanding to 2020 and beyond.

Those four priorities are, first, to increase the share of revenues derived from new geographic markets and, second, to lift the proportion of sales from digital media still further. Third, the group then wants to expand its presence in data investment management. The company wants to own the means – the technical assets – by which it can gather data, analyse audience sentiment and target advertising on the back of it. And, fourth, WPP wants to achieve what Sorrell calls greater 'horizontality'. In practice, this lateral thinking involves greater internal co-ordination in two broad areas. First, more clients are relying on unified global teams drawn from across WPP firms. Second, WPP's country and regional managers are being encouraged to pursue intra-firm co-operation, hiring and acquisition strategies in different parts of the world.

When it comes to geographic markets, WPP expects GDP from new markets to grow from $21 billion to $31 billion by the end of the decade. In order to tap into that growth, Sorrell has set a target to increase the group's share of revenues from faster-growing markets to 40–45 per cent of the total in 2020, compared with just over 30 per cent in 2013.

'There are a lot of grey swans, black swans or whatever you want to call them,' he admits. 'There is economic uncertainty in the eurozone, turmoil in the Middle East, a hard or soft landing in some BRIC economies and how to pay off the US debt. In addition, there is the Russian–Ukraine situation and, perennially, Gaza. Add to that the 2014 Hong Kong demonstrations and the Ebola outbreak.'

But he adds: 'There is some potentially good news coming if an agreement on sanctions (and, from a personal point of view, recognition of Israel) is reached with Iran. If Iran, which is 80 million people, becomes a market that is included in world affairs rather than excluded, that will be good news. The same goes for Cuba. We are seeing countries such as Myanmar open up. There are big growth opportunities in Africa, although it's very fragmented and markets such as Nigeria are difficult to penetrate. In the Middle East, we've seen Saudi Arabia grow very strongly. On China and Asia more broadly, I'm bullish and India could get better under the Modi regime.'

Sorrell thinks and speaks in a broad geo-political sweep because WPP's clients are focused increasingly on brand marketing and advertising spend in faster-growing markets, whilst working with clients in more mature markets such as Western Europe to tailor ad-spend to maintain their brand share. Given that advertising and marketing spending tend to track GDP growth, there is an expectation that increased exposure to fast-growth markets will offset any slowdown elsewhere.

Alongside new market growth, WPP is focusing its second strategic goal on increasing its exposure to digital and new media. By 2020 the group aims to increase its share of revenues from new media to 40–45 per cent of the total, compared with 35 per cent in 2013. Part of that growth will be derived from increasing Internet usage, with 48 per cent of the world population expected to be online by 2017, compared with 32 per cent in 2013. By the end of the decade, advertisers hope to be able to reach half of the world population through the World Wide Web.

'The class graduating from Harvard today is probably the first generation that spent its life from the day they popped their head out of the womb with the web, so their behaviour and attitude is bound to be totally different to you or me,' says Sorrell. 'We have got to be ready to target them on the devices that they use.'

WPP's media investment management business, GroupM, predicts that the mobile advertising floodgates are about to open. Half of Facebook's global advertising revenue is now mobile and Google predicts that 80 per cent of all its traffic will eventually come from that source. In some markets, such as China, mobile advertising could grow even faster. At China Mobile, the country's dominant wireless network, an estimated 400 million subscribers are already using data-heavy smartphones that lend themselves to online marketing. Such growth underlines why digital media buying has become more important to WPP. To capture mobile and online audiences, WPP has launched new operations such as Xaxis, a subsidiary operation to acquire digital advertising inventory and sell that space on to its clients.

Xaxis has become the world's largest programmatic media and technology platform, buying more than $800 million of audience-targeted media in thirty-three markets. Programmatic advertising uses automated software and algorithms to allocate advertising to media outlets with relevant space to sell. The business represents part of advertising's digital future, enabling computers to sell online inventory.

'An advertiser can buy a certain number of impressions on a website in advance at an agreed price and execute the order by computer,' according to *The Economist* in its 2014 advertising and technology report. 'The rise of real-time bidding [or programmatic buying] is important because it offers a glimpse of how other ad-supported media may change over time.'

Real-time bidding is one of the digital trends prompting WPP to spend around $3 billion of clients' money each year with Google – a company that Sorrell sometimes calls the 'frienemy'. Google is a friend in that it is a vital access point for advertisers to reach mass audiences around the world, opening up a giant market to match advertising to search requests. But Google also risks being the enemy because it takes most of the revenue from such search-related advertising, and because it diverts traffic and fees from outlets upon which companies such as WPP previously relied.

Over the next five years, the power of search engines and algorithms is likely to have a growing impact on advertising pricing as more devices such as televisions and even billboards become Internet-enabled. This is because the absolute cost per unit of advertising is much lower online, especially for mobile, in comparison to traditional print or broadcast advertising:

'The Internet is attractive to advertisers because you could shift a million dollars, notionally, from your TV budget to $100,000 of website spend,' says Sorrell. 'Not only did you think you were getting some efficiency gain, but you also got some money to tuck away into profit or some form of spending somewhere else. Because of fragmentation, I think the cost per advertising unit – if such a thing existed – for $100,000 of online spending has got even lower.'

This disequilibrium exposes one of the major challenges for digital media platforms. They are attracting audiences as readers or viewers migrate away from traditional media outlets. But the advertising spend required to reach those audiences remains far below the cost of a printed newspaper page or prime-time TV spot.

What this means is that media platforms are finding it harder to monetise advertising online, even though most of their audiences are now viewing content digitally. This is potentially good news for advertisers who want to reduce the per-viewer cost of placing an ad. But it is bad news for media outlets charging for advertising space, where they are now trying to sell according to total volume reach rather than the quality of the audience they offer.

Until relatively recently, for example, it was possible to buy every piece of advertising space on FT.com for a week for less than the cost of printing a full-page ad in the *Financial Times* on a single day. This reveals a time-lag in the way advertising is being sold. Big companies are not yet allocating as much of their total advertising spend to digital media as they are to traditional outlets. In the US, for example, the marketing services industry still allocated 23 per cent of its advertising budget to newspapers and magazines, even though consumers spent only 6 per cent of their media attention on those outlets. Free-to-air television is still a major magnet for advertising, and all forms of TV in developed markets are expected to continue to command 40 per cent of ad spending. This seems to indicate that advertising spending may yet continue to be allocated to television as long as it can attract large audiences. It is one reason why spot-advertising rates for event television such as the Super Bowl or European Champions League continue to rise.

But there is no room for complacency among newspaper publishers. They cannot promise the same 'big-event' audience as the TV networks, and have already suffered from the print-to-digital shift in three important advertising categories: property, recruitment and classifieds.

The need to interpret all of these trends, and to price advertising and marketing spend accordingly, explains in part why WPP has expanded its focus on data investment. Measurable marketing services – such as data investment management and digital research – are expected to account for a large part of total revenues in the years ahead. Data management will become even more important as advertisers try to harness 'big data' about consumer habits. By 2020, the amount of big data per head is expected to reach 5,200 gigabytes, compared to less than 260 gigabytes back in 2011. For the firms that can analyse and interpret such data, there is likely to be significant competitive advantage.

WPP is thus investing significant sums in data management to collect, interpret and combine data. By doing so, it hopes to provide advertisers with the audience measurement tools needed to enhance their marketing return on investment. The largest of those advertisers – the global corporations with huge marketing budgets – increasingly want to harness data analysis, and how it is applied to their media spend, to work with a single client team for all of their advertising and marketing. This trend has shaped the fourth strategic priority for WPP: the growth of 'horizontality'.

Of WPP's global business, about a third, or $6 billion of revenue, is now derived from teams from across the business that serve global clients. Among more than forty horizontal client teams, 'Team Detroit' manages the global Ford account, drawing on experts from WPP firms such as JWT, Hill + Knowlton and Burson-Marsteller. Similarly, a global team drawn from different firms manages the Colgate account, known as Red Fuse.

'Clients want the best people working on their business and they don't care where they come from,' says Sorrell. 'I think the way forward is for our people to be running clients not separate firms within our network. It simplifies the client relationship, removes needless duplication and means we can adapt to the demands of procurement officers.'

The WPP chief executive is not particularly enthused by the rising power of procurement departments when it comes to advertising and marketing spend. Since the debt crisis of 2008–10, the finance departments of many large clients have gained the upper hand over marketing directors, which is making companies more risk averse when it comes to advertising spend. That in turn is forcing marketing services groups such as WPP to focus on growth markets, on delivering their exposure to digital media – without ignoring high-value analogue platforms – whilst expanding their data management capabilities, and pursuing clients with multi-disciplinary global teams.

The pressure to achieve economies of scale – both in serving clients and reaching digital audiences – has also raised expectations of consolidation across the advertising industry. In 2014, that trend was highlighted by the aborted merger of Publicis and Omnicom Group ('POG', as Sorrell describes it), the US and French rivals. Sorrell believes it was 'doomed to failure' because the respective chief executives could not work out a structure for integrating or managing the two marketing giants: 'They hadn't really thought it through on a governance and cultural basis, quite apart from even more important issues such as the benefits for clients or benefits for their own people.'

In a people-centric business in 111 countries, WPP's chief executive sees one of his biggest challenges over the next few years to be identifying, recruiting and retaining the best people to steer his network of firms through the coming ad-market transformation. The period to 2020 is expected to be characterised by further audience fragmentation, in which traditional print and broadcast outlets risk losing their advertising appeal; new devices determine the content and distribution of next-generation marketing; and growth markets attract a greater share of global ad-spending.

'As we enter this period, success will be determined by having the very best people running your global client teams, and the very best minds working out how to manage the digital transition,' Sorrell argues. 'But the problem is that good people are difficult. Still, I'd rather have good people who are argumentative and hard to manage, rather than average people who are easy to deal with.'

He cites Goldman Sachs and McKinsey as examples of firms that nurture and retain top talent. He wants to see WPP build a similar culture, in which everyone is partly rewarded – whether Madison Avenue's

Mad Men or digital maths-men – according to the overall performance of the group in relation to its key performance indicators of digital growth, fast-growing markets and horizontal client management:

'By 2020, this business will be defined by faster growth markets, more digital, more data and more horizontality,' he adds. 'Those are the four things we are focused on. If we succeed, they will help achieve our goal to be the world's dominant communications services advisor.'

Second opinion: the analysts' view

For most of its history, the advertising industry has thrived on managing the laws of supply and demand. Successful firms made money by supplying creative campaigns to businesses that had to advertise to drive consumer demand. Agencies also satisfied the demand for revenues via media outlets with a life-dependency linked to the supply of advertising.

The Internet has turned the supply-and-demand equation upside down. In a digital world a potentially limitless amount of ad-space exists. As a result, the advertising cost-per-user is declining. In print media, advertising prices have fallen in line with circulation decline. Large companies, the bedrock of advertising, can now create and distribute their own marketing materials. Automated or programmatic buying is accounting for a growing proportion of ad spending.

The upheaval poses a major challenge for all advertising and marketing companies, WPP among them. In 2014, Sir Martin Sorrell told analysts: 'It pays to be paranoid.' He's right to be so.

Over the years, WPP has balanced its advertising exposure by expanding in specialist communications, public relations and consultancy. Its global revenue mix has offered a further protection against volatility in any one market, driving organic sales growth that is greater than that of rivals Interpublic, Omnicom and Publicis. All these companies must now navigate the digital transition in such a way that the opportunities outweigh the threats.

WPP, along with its competitors, is building its presence in data investment management. It predicts that almost 20 per cent of all advertising spending will be digital by 2020. Most analysts and investors think that figure could be even higher, so they applaud WPP's target to lift digital revenues to 40–45 per cent of the total by the end of the decade. Given generally sluggish economic conditions in mature markets, notably Japan and Western Europe, WPP is also right to broaden its exposure to faster-growing markets such as China and Africa.

But the biggest challenge will be whether it can monetise the opaque world of programmatic advertising, which appears set for inexorable growth. This world is becoming more fragmented as players including Google and Facebook attract increasing ad-inventory. They, in turn, are forcing traditional agencies to become even more digital.

The art of acquiring online advertising inventory, combining it with technology data and packaging it as a product to resell is far removed from the creative genius for which advertising types were previously known. But the incentive is clear. Digital is driving advertising demand. As the costs of data collection go down, margins should be enhanced rather than inhibited. If WPP can succeed in enhancing margins in a period of seismic industry change, it may emerge as a winner from the digital revolution.

Mark Schwab, Star Alliance

....

Total revenues of member airlines: $170.3 billion
Operating profit margin: N/A
Number of employees: 408,998
Number of markets served: 193

....

The chief executive of the world's first and largest airline alliance
entered the aviation industry as a manager for Pan American
Airways in 1975, joining the company as a junior country executive
in Brazil. He started work in Rio de Janeiro after studying Latin
American Affairs at the University of Virginia, Charlottesville. His
Pan Am role led to postings with Eastern, American Airlines,
US Airways and United, one of the founder members of Star.
His aviation career means he has spent most of his working life
outside the US. At United, he was Senior Vice President Alliances,
serving on the management board of Star. He became CEO
of Star in 2012, succeeding Jaan Albrecht, currently head of
Austrian Airlines.

By the end of the decade, Mark Schwab hopes to have no white spots and a more unified approach to blankets. For the chief executive of the Star Alliance, white spots and blankets represent two extremes of the challenges facing the world's first and largest alliance of international airlines. The family of more than two dozen carriers, accounting for a third of all commercial aviation, is seeking to address gaps – or 'white spots' – in its network of 22,000 daily flights to 195 countries. On those flights, it is seeking savings through more efficient procurement of everything from kerosene to in-flight linen.

Given the global reach and multinational membership of Star, the airline network is a barometer of the health of air travel, a sector dependent on business and consumer confidence. To maximise the returns on passenger demand, Schwab and his team must ensure that the alliance covers every corner of the globe.

'Our terminology at Star about where we go to recruit new carriers is to focus on the white spots. You look at a map of the world and identify the markets that we do not fully serve,' says Schwab. 'We have one white spot in Russia, and there is not an immediate obvious answer to that one. We addressed another white spot in 2014 with Air India joining Star – we were lacking domestic connectivity and a home base there – and we are now addressing Brazil. We have to rebuild our presence there because it is the fifth-largest domestic aviation market in the world, and represents about 40 per cent of the total Latin American market.'

The white spot in India has been an issue for several years. It was finally solved three years after the 2011 merger and far-reaching restructuring of Air India and Indian Airlines. The Indian carrier was admitted to Star after investing heavily in modernising its fleet and improving its service to customers. Before that investment it could not guarantee the service quality and inter-connectivity for passengers demanded by Star.

Mark Schwab and his team based at Frankfurt Airport hope to deliver efficiency savings among new and existing alliance members over the next five years. Although its members generate billions of dollars a year in revenue from connecting passengers on flights to 1,300 airports, the alliance has not been able to extract the same sort of savings from its federal structure compared with those of airlines that take over smaller rivals or enter into equity-sharing partnerships.

'The one area that we have been less successful has been delivering more value by joining purchasing activities,' says Schwab, a forty-year veteran of the aviation industry. 'We have been successful in purchasing commodities like jet fuel, but less so in purchasing articles that come into close contact with customers. Take blankets; you'd say "well a blanket is a blanket", but they come in all shapes and sizes, thickness and thinness. You multiply the cost of purchasing across twenty-seven carriers, and that's a significant variable overhead. All the alliances in our industry are still trying to figure out how to capture more value.'

The Star Alliance, established in 1997, competes with the **one**world alliance dominated by rivals including British Airways and American Airlines, as well as the SkyTeam network led by Air France KLM. Together, the three global alliances account for about 60 per cent of the world's airline travel, which is expected to grow at 5 per cent each year to 2020.

Schwab tracks that growth against a chart taped to his desk at Star headquarters, where each meeting room is named after a major city served by the alliance. The chart depicts per capita GDP on one axis and airline trips per year on the other.

'What you see is that below $5,000 per capita GDP there is virtually no air travel,' he explains. 'The minute you pass the $5,000-mark, you go to one trip per year and so on. To me, that chart explains why everybody is so interested in China and India. As they cross that mark, with a billion-plus people and the size of their land mass, all of a sudden you are going to end up with air-travel markets that are bigger than the very mature US market.'

Between 2015 and 2020, the largest rise in passenger demand is expected to come from the Asia Pacific region, which industry forecasters expect to expand by more than 6 per cent annually, compared with 2.3 per cent in North America and 3.5 per cent within Europe.

'In the coming years you will see increased focus on our part to developing markets,' says Schwab. 'We may have a couple more members in those geographies that are rapidly growing. I would predict that some carriers may leave and be replaced by other carriers. That's natural evolution.

'By 2020 we will be past our twenty-year mark. We will aim to consolidate and maximise revenue opportunities in all the most important markets in the world. And I think we will be providing many more centralised services to cut costs for our carriers. That is something that our members and their CEOs are expecting of us.'

By the end of the current decade, most of the aircraft and several of the airlines that dominated the industry when Schwab first joined Pan Am in the 1970s will be consigned to the history books. The thin margins and high operating costs of the airline industry have long taken their toll on carriers unable to compete. Pan Am, says Schwab, was pushed into bankruptcy by a combination of the financial burden that came with being the launch customer for the original Boeing 747 jumbo jet, the failed attempt to build a domestic network to rival United and American, and the economic slowdown that accompanied the first Gulf War.

While famous flag-carriers failed to survive, their executives had significant value to rivals seeking to expand, Schwab among them. After leaving Pan Am, he subsequently worked at American Airlines on its integration of Eastern Airlines' network in Latin America, before joining United to run its operations out of London and then US Airways as it expanded into Europe. He re-joined United, spending nine years heading its operations in Japan, before running its alliances department as the carrier embarked on its mega-merger of 2010 with Continental.

When Jaan Albrecht, then CEO of the Star Alliance, was appointed chief executive of Austrian Airlines, Schwab took over at the network. The airline veteran puts the longevity and dominance of alliances down to historic restrictions on cross-border mergers in many parts of the world: 'That is exactly why the alliances were created. Cross-border mergers were completely non-existent back in the nineties. Mergers are difficult in any industry and particularly hard with airlines. You have got to put labour agreements together, as well as different corporate and operating cultures.

'Instead, with Star and at the other alliances, a way was found to combine the right networks, build revenues and deliver enormous savings on driving efficiency from things such as unified IT systems. But there is more to be done to secure the full potential of these networks.'

Over the coming years, Schwab sees the potential for more joint ventures between alliance members to drive savings and ticketing revenue from particular routes, such as the United partnership with ANA of Japan on the Pacific route: 'They're capturing the next level of value through co-ordination of their pricing activities, their scheduling, and their go-to-market strategies – going to big corporate accounts or travel agents as a unit instead of separate entities.'

He also anticipates a narrowing in the cost differential, at least in the North American market, between legacy US carriers such as United and American and the low-cost carriers (LCCs), including Southwest and Jet Blue. This competitive convergence follows the major restructuring of several US mega-carriers, achieved partly through Chapter 11 bankruptcy proceedings that allowed them to cut labour costs. At the same time, the LCCs have matured and been forced to agree terms and conditions that have inflated their labour costs.

In spite of this cost-convergence, which the Star CEO expects to be replicated in Europe, LCCs have remained outside the alliances. Carriers from Ryanair and easyJet in the UK to Southwest in the US have refused to join or scoffed at the revenue benefits of being affiliated to one of the big three. Schwab attributes their isolationism to a business model that has eschewed two fundamental principles of the alliance world: business class travel and inter-airline connections. 'Our service offering is incompatible with the LCCs; it just doesn't work,' says Schwab. Products such as global connectivity, premier customer traffic, lounges, through check-in on different airlines and priority baggage delivery are a rarity in the LCC market.

But two new phenomena are emerging that may blur the distinction between the LCCs and the full-service airlines. First, the LCCs – even notoriously unfriendly Ryanair – are targeting business travellers with the promise of better service treatment. And low-cost airlines that previously operated only point-to-point routes are beginning to mimic the alliance model of connecting passengers to multiple destinations on their networks.

'The model is changing from both sides,' says Schwab. 'Some LCCs are becoming hybrid carriers by offering more and better services. And legacy carriers are changing their offering, because of cost pressures and the need to compete with the onslaught that is coming at them.'

The big three alliances are trying to respond with cost savings and service improvements, particularly shorter transfer times and better airport facilities. Star regards London Heathrow's Queen's Terminal, replacing the decrepit Terminal 2, as a statement of intent about its future customer service approach. All twenty-two Star members that operate out of Heathrow will, for the first time, be based at the same terminal. Schwab was first shown conceptual drawings of the new terminal by Heathrow's airport operator in 1998 – sixteen years before it eventually opened. 'What frustrates us is when airports go out and hire one of the big architectural firms to design them a pretty building but without thinking about the customer experience in connecting from one airline to another,' he says. Schwab believes airlines should be heavily involved in terminal design to ensure shorter connections, better lounges and easier check-in procedures.

'Any time we hear about a new airport or a new terminal project anywhere in our network of 1,300 cities, we get on a plane as quickly as we can to talk to the airport company to encourage them to consider connection services.'

In future, Star would like to see greater co-ordination among airports on border formalities. Of the complaints from passengers, government controls and lengthy passport queues are among the most frequent calls for change. Schwab describes a global standard for passport processing and managing border entry as an enormous opportunity for the industry, adding: 'I think alliances can help and will help find standards and solutions.'

Although there have been few new airports built in Europe or North America in the past generation, Schwab says that the Asian tiger economies have shown what can be achieved with better airport facilities. In the nine years that he spent leading United's operations in Japan, the airline moved to new airports or new terminal buildings in thirteen of the fifteen cities it served in the region. Whilst the planners dithered over

Heathrow's Terminal 5 and other European infrastructural projects, new airports or terminals were opened in Beijing, Shanghai, Tokyo, Seoul, Taipei, Bangkok and Singapore, among others.

At the same time, mega-hubs sprang up in the Middle East Gulf States, posing a new and major challenge to legacy European airports in particular. But Star has declined to invite any of the powerful new Gulf carriers such as Emirates or Etihad to join its club because Schwab thinks the benefits would flow one way only: 'The reason we are not recruiting a Gulf carrier to join Star is because we don't need to. Our carriers already provide services to every country in the Gulf region, so we wouldn't actually add anything to our network. The other principle behind Star is that every member brings a strong and attractive home market for other members to access. What would you define as the home market of Dubai or Doha? It's a tiny domestic market. We see a big advantage for them, accessing our 200 million frequent fliers. But in return we would get a commercial imbalance.'

So Star is responding by focusing on route networks that promise mutual benefit to its members. China could be a major test bed for such future co-operation. In 2013, EVA Air of Taiwan joined Star, complementing a line-up of airlines that includes Shenzhen Airlines and Air China.

'Ten years ago, there was not a single flight between the PRC and Taiwan. If you wanted to get there you would have to go via Hong Kong, Seoul or Tokyo. Right now they are operating 500 flights a week across the straits. Both governments are looking to triple that in coming years.'

Such growth is a symptom of the predicted expansion in inter-Asian air travel by 2020. US demand is expected to grow relatively slowly while Europe is expected to see continued expansion of low-cost short-haul traffic, with an increasing shift towards what Schwab calls 'hybridisation' among airlines. Latin America is forecast to show double-digit expansion in some countries. Africa is the exception to the trend. Poor or under-invested airport infrastructure is holding back the continent's air travel industry. Given the deep-seated economic challenges and other pressing investment priorities in many African nations, the continent's commercial aviation industry could take decades to modernise fully.

Where growth exists, Star hopes to capitalise on it with greater co-ordination between its member airlines, which are divided into tiers depending on their size and contributions to shared synergies. Drawing its inspiration from astronomy, each tier is named after a different constellation, separating the mega-carriers – the largest of which has a thousand aircraft – from the airline minnows. The smallest airline in Star has just fifteen planes.

Whatever their size, the Star CEO says the alliance must deliver both higher revenue synergies and greater cost savings wherever possible. He aims to do this through greater co-development of alliance strategies, greater use of passenger data information and by building a series of tools – especially in IT – to become more cost-efficient.

In a crisis, the alliance is expected to work swiftly to minimise the impact on passengers. Over the course of its history, three Star carriers have gone bust: Varig of Brazil, Ansett of Australia and Spanair of Spain. Others have been heavily restructured, such as SAS of Scandinavia and United, following bankruptcy protection. Schwab says Star is not a safety net for underperforming carriers, and will not bail out those facing problems. But the alliance does attempt to protect passenger interests. If one carrier faces major disruption – as a result of industrial action or technical problems – passengers can be re-routed or offered alternative flights with other member airlines.

In the medium term, Star aims to increase its flight network, benefits to frequent fliers and service efficiencies, driven mainly by air traffic growth in emerging markets. But it warns that it cannot change the travelling experience on its own, particularly when airlines depend upon airport infrastructure or fragmented air traffic control systems that – in Europe at least – require reform. That is why Star is among the airline groups urging European policymakers to create a 'single European sky' that combines continued investment in infrastructure on the ground and in the air to keep up with global industry standards.

In spite of sluggish growth prospects in Europe and the mature nature of the North American market, Schwab remains optimistic that Star can withstand competition from LCCs and other alliances; deal with constrained airport capacity; and improve service among carriers ranging from Adria Airways at one end of the size-spectrum to Lufthansa and United at the other.

The airline industry remains fragile and highly exposed to consumer demand. But those carriers that can cut costs while maintaining service standards should be equipped to navigate most forms of economic turbulence.

'We are growing our total capacity at around 5 per cent every year, and with it our service to members,' says the Star CEO. 'Unless there is some major shock to the global system, this is a direction of travel that is going to continue cruising along.'

Second opinion: the analysts' view

The methodology used to calculate airline industry profits sometimes resembles an air traffic control chart. Load factors and yields are determined by CASM (cost per available seat mile) along with RPKs (passenger revenue per available seat kilometre). And because of differences in routes, aircraft and ticket demand, profitability may depend on SLA TRESM (stage length adjusted total revenue per equivalent seat mile).

Add to those fuel costs, fleet renewal, aircraft depreciation, capacity adjustments, landing charges and differing labour agreements for pilots and crew, and predicting mid-term performance gets trickier still. No wonder that airline industry analysts at Barclays in New York warn: 'We might be forced to make substantial and frequent changes to our profit expectations, targets, and recommendations' if assumptions on industry capacity, labour issues or geo-political events change.

Given high costs and operating uncertainty, it should also be no surprise that most airlines operate at relatively low margins. Net profit margins at United Airlines, a key member of the Star Alliance, are expected to average less than 6 per cent on annual revenues of about $40 billion over the 2013–16 period. At Lufthansa, its sister carrier in Star, margins are even tighter due to surplus capacity and expensive labour disputes.

Profitability may be enhanced in the coming years by the beneficial impact of cheaper fuel, the introduction of more economical aircraft and reduced labour costs. The challenge for airlines is how to manage costs downwards while also introducing new aircraft that will deliver a better return on investment. Boeing, the US aircraft manufacturer, predicts that more than 36,000 new aircraft with a total value of $5.2 trillion will be ordered in the 2013–33 period – of which about 40 per cent will be to replace old planes. But the majority will be for incremental market expansion. Most of that expansion is expected to take place in the Asia Pacific region, and particularly in China. That is why Star and the other alliances are building their presence in the region. Members of Star – including Air China and EVA of Taiwan – now operate more than 4,000 daily flights to, from and within the Asia Pacific region.

To maximise profitability, alliance members must extract sufficient revenue-sharing opportunities to offset the cost of increased competition in high-growth markets, and to absorb the legacy costs of operating in slower-growth high-volume markets including the US and Europe.

Lower fuel charges following the 2014 oil price collapse will help, as should ancillary revenues from frequent flier programmes, on-board sales and baggage charges. It remains to be seen whether that will be sufficient to withstand the threat posed by low-cost carriers at one end of the market and premium-orientated Gulf carriers at the other.

Of those Gulf carriers, Qatar Airways signalled its ambition to challenge Star by acquiring, in January 2015, a near 10 per cent stake in International Airlines Group, the parent of British Airways and Iberia. Its share acquisition came shortly after IAG made a takeover offer for Aer Lingus of Ireland, which could create a more vertically integrated group of carriers within **one**world, the main competitor to the Star Alliance.

Still, alliance members without the appetite or spending power for takeovers or equity acquisitions believe that by sticking together they are more likely to reach cruising altitude in revenue and profit terms. Short of abandoning a loose federal structure for mergers and acquisitions, they probably have little choice. But given recent economic volatility and geo-political tensions, their journey towards savings and great profitability is likely to be a turbulent one.

Li Shufu, Zhejiang Geely Holding Group

Annual revenues – Geely: $4.6 billion; **Volvo:** $15.4 billion
Operating profit margin – Geely Auto: 9%; **Volvo:** 1.6%
Number of employees – Geely/ZGH: 17,000; **Volvo:** 23,000
Number of markets served – Geely: 55; **Volvo:** 100+
Headquarters: Hangzhou; Gothenburg

Li Shufu was named one of the 'Top 10 Private Entrepreneurs in China' by Ernst & Young following the 2010 acquisition of Volvo Car Corporation by Zhejiang Geely Holding Group, the Chinese automotive group that he founded in 1997. The takeover marked a milestone for the softly spoken billionaire, born in 1963 in Taizhou, Zhejiang province. He began his business career in the mid-1980s, producing fridge components, after graduating with a degree in Management Engineering from Harbin University of Science and Technology. He also has a PhD in Mechanical Engineering from Yanshan University. As chairman of both Volvo Cars and Geely Auto, he also serves as vice chairman of the China Association of Automobile Manufacturers. Li is a member of the Chinese People's Political Consultative Conference.

Few politicians can resist a car factory when they want to stress the importance of manufacturing. From Detroit to Dagenham, automotive production lines represent an easy photo opportunity for any party leader urging investment and growth. The tactic is not confined to mature democracies. It is equally true in China. In late 2014, Premier Li Keqiang used a visit to Zhejiang province to demand 'new growth engines' and more 'created-in-China' products. After emphasising his pro-growth credentials, the Chinese premier posed for the obligatory car-plant picture alongside Li, chairman of Zhejiang Geely Holding Group, the country's largest privately owned car-maker.

In the automotive industry, there is no greater growth engine than China, and few companies more ambitious than Zhejiang Geely. In 2010, the company – based in the provincial capital of Hangzhou – made international headlines with an audacious $1.8 billion takeover of Volvo Cars. By acquiring the famous Swedish brand from Ford Motor Company, Zhejiang Geely became the first Chinese group to acquire one of the world's leading premium brands.

The acquisition of Volvo was certainly a coup for the boy from the coastal city of Taizhou, a one-time photography enthusiast and occasional poet. It also symbolised the rapid rise of China as a serious player in global mergers and acquisitions. Companies that barely existed a generation ago were able to acquire much older household names. In the late 1980s, when Volvo was celebrating its sixtieth anniversary, Li was making refrigerator parts in Zhejiang province. Today, he is Volvo's chairman.

In China, it is unsurprising that an entrepreneur can jump within a decade from one industry to another. In a country of few indigenous brands at the turn of the millennium, entrepreneurs created fast-growing businesses in a period of great experimentation. They tried their luck in one industry before finding the right formula, access to capital and market opportunity in another. Hence, Li moved from refrigerators to motorcycles and ultimately to car-making with the 1997 launch of Geely Auto, the domestic brand that he founded. Since then, after a painful learning curve in automotive quality and productivity, Geely Auto has become one of China's leading car exporters. Its chairman is ranked as one of the top ten private entrepreneurs in China.

Although Geely Auto remains a relatively modest player compared with more established global auto manufacturers, generating revenues of about 30 billion remnimbi ($4.9 billion), its growth reflects the extraordinary expansion of the Chinese market. A company that did not even exist in the mid-1990s now sells almost 550,000 cars a year, a third of which are exported. At 9 per cent, its profit margins rank above companies that are much older and bigger. By revenue, Volvo is more than three times larger than its Chinese sibling, at SKr122 billion ($14.8 billion) and with an operating profit of almost SKr2 billion ($242 million) in the 2013 financial year. Volvo's aim is to deliver the products and market expansion that will generate an 8 per cent profit margin by 2020.

Li, who holds a PhD in mechanical engineering, is not satisfied with these results. He believes both Geely Auto and Volvo Cars should be capable of more rapid growth, wider market penetration and improved profitability. He sees plenty of room for growth in the global market for new cars, expecting annual unit sales to reach 95 million by 2020. By then, China is likely to have consolidated its position as the world's largest market, accounting for close to 30 million of the world's new car sales. The chairman of Geely Auto and Volvo wants his two brands to represent about 2 million units of that global total. Volvo has been set a target of reaching more than 800,000 units, with the remainder coming from its Chinese sister company.

In pursuing those targets, Li insists that the profit motive is not his main driving force: 'I think there are two types of enterprise. One is purely focused on commercial gains and pursues profit as a single target,' he says. 'The other type is very much focused on what's behind and driving the commercial side of the business – and that's the need to innovate in every part of the business, to deliver products that are more environmentally friendly, to sustain jobs and investment, and deliver a broader societal benefit. If you ask me what school I'm in, it's the latter.'

For any student of the auto industry, Volvo would rank as one of the brands meeting Li's aspiration of environmental consciousness and energy efficiency. Those two attributes are highly valued in China, where chronic pollution and congestion are expected to be two of the issues tackled in the thirteenth five-year plan, the Communist Party's policy programme for 2016–20.

Volvo's leadership in low-emission technologies and safety systems and its early embrace of sustainability were powerful attractions for the Zhejiang Geely chairman, who began tracking the Swedish company almost a decade before he made an offer to Ford. The US auto giant was ready to sell because it needed cash. Ford had avoided the fate of rivals GM and Chrysler, which both filed for bankruptcy protection following the financial crash, by mortgaging every plant in its portfolio. It may have escaped Chapter 11, but it ended up with borrowings of more than $20 billion.

To pay down that debt, a 'For Sale' sign was hoisted on numerous Ford assets, among them its premium European car brands: Jaguar, Land Rover and Volvo. In a first for the auto industry, all three were snapped up by emerging market players. Tata Motors of India acquired the combined Jaguar Land Rover, whilst Zhejiang Geely – a company few people in Sweden had ever heard of – entered into exclusive talks with a view to acquiring Volvo Cars.

In 2015, Geely will celebrate the fifth anniversary of that acquisition. As it approaches that milestone, Chairman Li summarises the strategy for Volvo Cars under four headings: 'First, Volvo must harness the freedom that comes from being a standalone and independent company that can be truly global, and which can make decisions through its own governance structure. That kind of freedom has never been there before.'

He hints that Volvo was constrained within Ford, where it had to jostle for investment with other larger parts of the 'Blue Oval'. And he contends that the Swedish brand was not master of its own destiny when it was previously part of the larger AB Volvo commercial vehicles, construction equipment, marine power and industrial engines group. At a 2010 press conference to announce the acquisition of Volvo Cars, Chairman Li vowed to 'unleash the tiger' in the company. Today, he expresses that ambition more soberly: 'Our second clear strategic objective is to get Volvo where it used to be, which is head to head with Mercedes and other premium German brands. We don't want it to be seen as less premium.

'Thirdly, we want Volvo to benefit from the support of a shareholder that is an insider and an expert on the biggest auto market in the world.

'And lastly, the fourth area of opportunity is to unlock synergies with Volvo's brother-company, Geely Auto. We can achieve economies of scale from areas of mutual market knowledge and shared technologies in certain areas. These four strategic objectives are all inter-dependent. Without freedom, Volvo would find it harder to survive as a company. Without the other benefits, its growth would be harder to guarantee.'

Volvo's growth plan depends crucially on China. For the first time, the company has started full-scale assembly outside Europe: its inaugural Chinese car plant in Chengdu has an installed capacity to produce about 125,000 cars per year. It is also producing engines in Zhangjiakou, in the greater Beijing area, with a 300,000-unit annual capacity, whilst conducting research and development at a new centre in Shanghai.

The result is already visible in Volvo sales, which climbed more than 40 per cent in China in 2014, overtaking the US to become the brand's single largest market. Volvo, which retains a fiercely independent culture and guards its technology closely, knows it must succeed in China. Its long-term target is to sell 200,000 cars in China a year, which will require a greatly expanded dealer network and output from a second car plant in Daqing.

Volvo and Geely are united on their shared vision for China. But their chairman has had to use all his powers of persuasion to win over his Swedish workforce. Given the proud independence of the company, Li has gone out of his way to soothe Scandinavian sensitivities. Ever since buying the business he has intoned, 'Volvo is Volvo, and Geely is Geely'. Echoing China's 'one country, two systems' mantra for Hong Kong, Li has insisted that the two brands are clearly differentiated in the eyes of the customer and are managed completely separately. Yet both the Swedes and the Chinese know that they cannot operate in isolation, particularly given the costs and risks involved in developing new automotive technologies. This is leading to co-operation on specific projects that promise to deliver increased competitiveness, greater economies of scale and shared best practice.

Given Volvo's caution regarding brand overlap, Geely has now established a mechanism to explore co-operation at arm's length from both operating companies. The incubator is the so-called 'China-Europe Vehicle Technology' (CEVT) centre on the outskirts of Gothenburg, Volvo's home town. The purpose of the joint-venture project, employing a Chinese-Swedish workforce, is to develop shared vehicle architectures in the mid-size or C-car segment, both for Volvo and Geely. The centre will also be responsible for the initial development phase of new Geely vehicles, instilling European expertise and engineering skills into cars for the Chinese brand. The project aims to secure more co-operation between Volvo and Geely, without offending Swedish sensibilities over brand differentiation and proprietary technology. When Li tries to explain the balancing act of co-operation without compromising brand integrity, he grabs two small water bottles and gesticulates from one to the other:

'Technology is not like a resource-commodity. It's not like a tonne of gold that I benefit from just owning and have to keep captive to retain value. Technology is something that is continuing to develop and evolve.

'It is not the case that Geely gets Volvo technology and Volvo gets nothing in return. Both companies have their own IP and technology to offer. Volvo is also gaining finance, market expertise and a manufacturing presence in the world's largest market.

'Utilising the CEVT project, each brand can harness the most feasible technologies to suit their brand positioning and product. And if they need jointly developed technologies they can do that. I am confident that more and more leading technology will be created at the CEVT centre.'

New technology is central to Geely Auto's vision. Zhejiang Geely Holding, the parent company of both Volvo Cars and Geely Auto, recognises that indigenous Chinese brands are still not competitive in relation to European or Japanese competitors in terms of product quality, design and reliability. So Li expects the Gothenburg technology centre to deliver technologies and vehicle architectures that will make Geely Auto more competitive.

These technologies could include ultra-low-emission electric cars and more efficient engines, as well as the 'Compact Modular Architecture' (CMA) that will be used by Volvo as well as Geely Auto. Some of these technologies will also be used in future by the London Taxi Company, the iconic manufacturer of London black cabs which Zhejiang Geely rescued from bankruptcy in 2013. Given that London Mayor Boris Johnson has mandated that from 2018 all new taxis must have zero-emission capabilities, London Taxi is turning to its Chinese parent for the technology to address such requirements.

But Li is realistic about the timeframe in which the overall group will reap the dividends: 'If you're talking about Geely Auto, it will take five years to be internationally competitive. With more competitive technology we could add another 100,000–200,000 units per year to the Geely Auto total, taking the total to around 600,000 units. On top of that, there is scope to sell a further 250,000 cars each year, thanks entirely to the CMA platform developed with Volvo.

'If we could achieve that scale without sacrificing margins that would be the way to go. We must also make this brand more international. I would like to see a 50–50 split of exports to domestic sales in five years' time, compared with a third to two-thirds at present.'

As part of that effort, Geely Auto has established an international sales presence in markets such as Egypt, Ukraine and Saudi Arabia – markets where some other manufacturers fear to tread – and also entered the Brazilian market in 2014. The company aims to build a presence across the Mercosur region – beyond Brazil to include Argentina, Bolivia, Paraguay, Uruguay and Venezuela – with vehicles assembled in a factory near Montevideo.

Li believes his portfolio of auto companies can realise their strategic goals – higher volumes, improved profitability and wider consumer appeal – because they are more entrepreneurial than most of their Chinese competitors, many of which are state-owned. These state-owned Chinese companies, he argues, are not incentivised to deliver the same rates of growth, the same shareholder returns, as privately held groups. This, he says, means they are more risk averse and less likely to make bold acquisitions.

'Geely won't be unique but I don't expect to see large-scale acquisitions by Chinese companies in the next five years. Although we have seen Dongfeng has taken a stake in PSA Peugeot Citroën, my view is that the auto industry is too complex to see a lot of Chinese acquisitions.' Most state-owned enterprises, Li maintains, do not operate to the same value-creation and long-term sustainability standards as Western companies. Li is also vice chairman of the China Association of Automobile Manufacturers, the trade body representing all domestic car-makers, and he points to state ownership as being unhelpful in the car industry:

'China is unique in the history of the industry with most auto businesses being state-owned, and for many years private investment was banned in this area with a few exceptions. This is an industry that requires entrepreneurship to continue developing. But this does not seem to be the philosophy of most Chinese car companies.

'When it comes to expansion by state-owned enterprises, I think international expansion will be more viable in areas such as oil and gas and utilities. In these industries, state ownership delivers certain strengths. But it is just not advantageous in the auto sector.'

His intervention reflects a strong interest in public policy. Li is a member of the Chinese People's Political Consultative Conference, the annual policy gathering at which delegates can submit proposals for legislative debate. At the 2013 CPPCC meeting, Li made proposals aimed at fiscal reform, support for private higher education, improved car safety standards and liberalisation of China's highly centralised taxi market.

Most controversially, he called for reform of the 'foreign-funded company law', claiming that it placed a significant burden on globalising Chinese companies that were acquiring international assets. Regulations in this area are geared to inward investment by foreign companies seeking to expand in China, rather than Chinese companies seeking to expand acquired brands in China. As a result, although Zhejiang Geely owns Volvo Cars outright, it has to treat its subsidiary as a joint venture partner involving lengthy approvals processes and obligations that do not apply to wholly Chinese assets.

Li's reform proposals form part of his vision for a more globalised and market-driven approach to China's corporate culture. He sees Zhejiang Geely, Volvo Cars and Geely Auto as symbols of how this corporate culture should work in future. Whilst maintaining separate brand identities and pursuing different market segments, they are increasingly sharing best practice and advanced technologies in areas such as vehicle development and clean-engine technology. He believes such technologies are vital to China's car industry if the country is to tackle chronic pollution in many of its cities.

'There is a clear policy that we should develop cleaner vehicles to meet the needs of Chinese society, and the products on offer should include pure electric, plug-in hybrids and alternative fuel cars. But before these technologies can be commercialised, we need to take a stand on fuel consumption and lower emissions in conventional cars – which we think must be comparable to the US and Europe in their standards.'

He also claims that Zhejiang Geely's automotive subsidiaries have the inside track on developing such engines and new products, taking a lead from the zero-emission technologies under development at Volvo. The trick will be to achieve economies of scale across the Geely group by deploying such technologies, without diluting the distinctive and premium-orientated customer appeal of the Volvo brand. Li says that Zhejiang Geely is playing its part in improving quality and lowering emissions in its domestic brand – learning from Volvo – but still needs the right policy environment to allow such entrepreneurialism to flourish. Here, Li reveals his true colours. As the billionaire founder and controlling shareholder of one of China's largest private manufacturers, he is impatient with protectionism or policy inertia designed to safeguard state-owned enterprise: 'I think that when it comes to innovation, building market share and harnessing global opportunities, you must let the market decide rather than leave it to government. State intervention does not allow Chinese companies to prosper because if you don't let the market decide, then the group of companies you are trying to protect will become weaker and weaker.'

Having acquired Volvo Cars from Ford, rescued the London Taxi Company, and put Geely Auto on a path to export growth, Li has a distinctly capitalist view of success over the next five years:

'Leave it to the market, and it will be consumers who then benefit,' he says. 'The companies that are fit will not only survive; they will thrive.'

Second opinion: the analysts' view

Zhejiang Geely Holding (ZGH) rather surprised the automotive world when towards the end of 2009 it announced it was acquiring Volvo Cars. Following in the footsteps of Tata and its acquisition of Jaguar Land Rover, Geely was the second company from the BRIC nations to acquire a premium branded automotive company at a time of general financial stress.

The world economy at that time, and the state of the automotive market, meant that ZGH was able to buy an iconic name at an attractive price. It was clear that none of the Western automotive manufacturers were a likely buyer as they were either cash-strapped or would not benefit from the addition of the Volvo brand to existing portfolios.

This meant that the Chinese did not have significant competing bids to overcome. For ZGH, the asset was doubly attractive as it could benefit from the significant investment Ford had made in Volvo during its ownership, applying some of its newly-acquired assets systems and technologies to its own Chinese domestic brand: Geely Automotive.

Notwithstanding the attractive price at which ZGH acquired Volvo, Geely did face challenges, and continues to do so. Volvo is regarded by some analysts as almost in a niche of its own as a brand, not directly competing against the big three German premium brands. Its reputation has been built on its attention to safety, although in recent years its model range has been revamped, bringing in a sportier image and a successful sports utility product range. How Geely positions the brand in both its traditional markets and in China, relative to other premium brands will be crucial. Where it should have an advantage relative to its competitors is in managing its dealer network in China, which has been problematic for foreign companies.

Scale is another challenge. Volvo has always been a small scale manufacturer and even its 2014 sales were less than half a million units. It is debatable whether production at this level can generate the cash needed to sustain the investment required for new model and engine development over the long term. Geely's stated aim to increase Volvo's annual volumes to 800,000 units is still modest relative to the Germans – in 2014 BMW reported sales of approximately 2 million units, Mercedes-Benz 1.74 million and Audi 1.74 million.

Given the very different product lines of Geely Automotive and Volvo, extracting synergies from the combination of the two companies will continue to need considerable planning.

ZGH has now owned Volvo for five years in which time it has grown sales and returned the company to profitability. It has also provided Volvo with new manufacturing facilities in China which, previously, would have been unattainable for the company and assists it in developing models for the fast growing Chinese market. Geely Auto, meanwhile, has benefited from access to areas of Volvo's technological expertise which, similarly, it would previously have found difficult to replicate by itself. The second five years of ownership by ZGH, a period which is arguably more challenging than the first five years, will be crucial in determining the long term success of Geely Automotive as a significant automotive company both for its own model range and attendant sales ambitions and for its continuing development of Volvo in a highly competitive marketplace both international and domestic.

If middle-class Chinese consumers continue to favour European premium brands, Volvo should do well. Domestic manufacturers including Geely could also overcome near-term challenges – and recent profit warnings – if overall Chinese car ownership continues to rise at 20 per cent annually, as it has since 2009. But that rests on assumptions that Chinese incomes and consumer confidence will remain robust. The whole auto industry hopes that is the case. As analysts at Morgan Stanley note: 'Without China the world is not growing.'

Kasper Rorsted, Henkel

Annual revenues: $19.5 billion
Operating profit margin: 16%
Number of employees: 47,000
Number of markets served: 80
Headquarters: Düsseldorf

The Danish technology executive became chief executive of
Henkel in 2008, three years after joining the German fast-moving
consumer goods group from Hewlett-Packard. He led HP's
European business for two years, appointed to that role after
seven years at Compaq from 1995–2002. Prior to Compaq,
he worked in sales and marketing at Oracle. His technology
background attracted Henkel, which he joined initially as executive
vice president of human resources, purchasing, information
technologies and infrastructure services. The graduate of
Copenhagen's International Business School, who also studied at
Harvard, is a non-executive board member at German media group
Bertelsmann, and Danfoss, the Danish engineering technology
business.

K asper Rorsted has a good view of the White Lady from his office window at the headquarters of Henkel. Thirty metres below, painted on the gable-end of a house, she stares perpetually over the Düsseldorf industrial complex that is home to Henkel, the global manufacturer of household goods, beauty-care products and adhesives. In the 1920s, the young woman in full-length dress and Florentine hat was the advertising symbol of Persil. Back then, the detergent was the flagship product of a business that today spans hundreds of consumer and industrial brands from Purex and Schwarzkopf to Loctite and Pritt.

Just as the White Lady symbolises Henkel's past, latter-day Henkel is on display in the chief executive's office. Instead of the normal C-suite trophies celebrating mergers and acquisitions, Kasper Rorsted gives pride of place to packets of Persil High Suds Gel, Vernel Aroma Therapy, Syoss Oleo Intense and Pattex Power Glue. Behind his desk, there is a neat metaphor for Henkel's future: a planet-shaped artwork comprising hundreds of multi-coloured balls – all of them seemingly in the air at once. From his top-floor office, the fifty-two-year-old Dane has spent seven years as CEO juggling the corporate demands of a business with some 200 plants, 47,000 employees and more than €16 billion ($18.8 billion) of annual revenues.

Rorsted has a near-term vision to lift those revenues to €20 billion ($23 billion) in 2016, of which half is expected to come from emerging markets. To achieve those goals, he has embarked on a strategy combining globalisation, bolt-on acquisitions, improved technologies and brand simplification.

'When we worked on the 2016 strategy, we identified three mega-trends. One was consolidation of the industry; the second one was a shift of growth to emerging markets; and the third one was to achieve sufficient operational excellence to withstand market volatility – whether political or currency or the speed-of-information. We had to ensure we would benefit from all these market changes, instead of having them as a threat.'

As it pursues that vision, Henkel has simultaneously expanded its presence in emerging markets, pressed ahead with an aggressive reduction in its brand portfolio and continued with acquisitions in sectors where it seeks market leadership.

'Today we have about 45 per cent of our business and 57 per cent of all our people in emerging markets. It is not just plants, but management and service structures, and we have opened seven R&D centres in these territories,' says the CEO.

The former head of Hewlett-Packard's European business, who first joined Henkel in 2005 before becoming CEO in 2008, also ordered a fundamental rethink of how the company used digital technology in its manufacturing processes, internal communications and customer engagement: 'When I first came here, we had overhead projectors. I hadn't seen an overhead projector since 1995, so it was interesting to see them again. But they have all gone. There is no difference to how we run the company today compared to an IT company. Everything is digital.'

Rorsted also adopted standard processes from HP after finding that Henkel was too fragmented and too German. Although its German roots meant Henkel was rigorously efficient in its production methods, the company for too long relied on the doctrine that what was best for its home market was best for the rest of the world. Describing today's operating processes as 'matters of discipline', he explains that Henkel has 'moved from being a German company with subsidiaries to become a much more global organisation where we don't use the term subsidiaries anymore'.

Each working day, 5,500 employees representing more than fifty nationalities file through the main gates in Düsseldorf, past a reception area where a bust of family founder Fritz Henkel is flanked by stands displaying the company's best-selling brands. The CEO says the Henkel family, which controls 59 per cent of the group's ordinary shares, is fully behind his corporate re-engineering.

Although the family has a longer-term view than most institutional shareholders, Rorsted argues that there is little distinction between family or public investors when it comes to their appetite for sustainable, long-term returns. He also rejects suggestions that family-controlled companies are risk averse or less willing to make transformative acquisitions than fully listed groups.

'I spent twenty years in American companies. I don't find that the board plays a different role, positive or negative, in a German or family-based company compared with a US one. I have not, as a CEO, felt restricted because we had a family shareholder. There are certain things we do in a different way, so when we do make a change within the organisation or [plan] restructuring, we might go about it in a different way than some American companies. But there has been zero restriction to what we have been doing within our organisation.'

He does, however, acknowledge that the family has greater emotional sensitivity than other shareholders concerning reputational issues. Given that the family name appears in small-print on many products, and in large-type on its buildings around the world, the Henkels and their descendants are justifiably concerned by any move that threatens long-term brand positioning. Even so, the supervisory board chaired by Simone Bagel-Trah, great-great-granddaughter of Fritz Henkel, has not objected to a wide-ranging cull of many brand-lines. In 2008, when Rorsted assumed the top job, Henkel had more than 1,000 brands. Today, the figure is down to 250, with another fifty earmarked for the chop.

'When we started the exercise back in 2008 it was then a more painful exercise because we needed to make the organisation understand the strategic imperative behind the decision,' he explains. 'And the imperative is you need to have strong brands, whether they are industrial or consumer [products] in order to be relevant in the market that you're in. The fewer brands that you have, the stronger your presence can be. In the beginning it was painful. Today, it's not something that people are worried about because they know that having billion-dollar brands is an important part of the company's success.'

In 2015, Henkel aims to have four billion-dollar brands, by revenue, with potentially two $2 billion brands. The case for rationalisation seems clear. Already, Henkel's top ten brands in beauty care account for 90 per cent of revenues in that area. In laundry and home care, the top ten brands account for 80 per cent of divisional sales. And the industrial adhesives business is two-and-a-half times the size of its nearest competitor, with Loctite as the market leader.

Yet simplification of the brand strategy has not prevented continued acquisitions. In 2014, the company spent almost a billion euros ($1.1 billion) on acquiring Spotless Group, the laundry specialist in stain removers and fabric dyes. And it paid a further €270 million ($306 million) for 'SexyHair', Alterna and Kenra to broaden its beauty-care portfolio.

'We need to do two things,' Rorsted says. 'We need to accelerate organic growth and accelerate acquisitions. We have acquired two companies in our fast-moving consumer goods area. But that does not indicate that the next up will be the industrial side. It is really the strategic fit that will drive the decision, rather than a sequence of whose turn is it to dance.'

Rorsted is also focused on strategic geographies in both mature and emerging markets. He would like to build a bigger presence in North America, where Henkel aims to narrow the margin and market-share gap between it and arch rival P&G.

'I think in the longer term we need to have a larger position in North America. We do approximately 17 per cent of our business in North America, and the US is still the largest economy in the world. This is not something I worry about every night. But if I look at it and ask where should we grow? There is still a lot of value to be captured in North America.'

In spite of challenging market conditions in Western Europe, particularly in southern parts of the eurozone, the company says it remains committed to the region where it was founded. But that does not mean that Henkel is relaxed about the cost base of the European Union. The chief executive acknowledges that few countries have benefited more than Germany from globalisation and the euro. Yet he is concerned about the potential impact of EU regulations on industrial competitiveness:

'There is no doubt that the more the single European market can evolve, the better it is for us. There is also no doubt that the EU has been pursuing regulations that are not always beneficial and which are not co-ordinated with individual countries.

'Without being political, I think David Cameron was quite right when he said, "I am not against the EU, but [think] that the EU needs to evolve and take care of bigger matters than the size of bananas and cucumbers". The EU has a tremendous opportunity. But it needs to find a role to play and not over-regulate the market.'

Given those concerns in Europe, Henkel is trying to leverage its strengths in mature markets and applying both product and customer expertise to other regions. The biggest focus of that leverage is on the group's emerging markets footprint. The company now has sixteen plants in China, one of which is the world's largest adhesives factory, near Shanghai. It has a production capacity of 430,000 tonnes a year. It has also expanded rapidly in Africa and the Middle East, where it has opened a regional innovation centre in Dubai. The CEO insists this emerging market expansion is not about exporting production and jobs from high- to low-cost parts of the world. Henkel does not export substantial volumes of products between continents. Instead, it opens plants close to market, and produces and sells goods that are adapted to local consumer demand.

Explaining what he means, Rorsted takes a packet of Persil from his windowsill and puts a gel-capsule on the desk.

'Take Persil,' he says. 'In Western Europe or the US, a consumer expects a number of things; one is cleanliness and the other is aroma. A piece of clothing is typically washed after being worn once. If you start going to Eastern Europe or the Middle East, a person is typically using his or her clothes three, four or five times. The primary objective of washing a piece of clothing is removing odour and making it clean because it is much dirtier. So we have to develop a different product for different markets.

'Take a dishwasher in Western Europe or the US; all the advertising is about how to make things shine. In Eastern Europe you load up your dishwasher with everything you have because you don't care if it's completely shiny. You care about whether all the stuff you put in, including your pots and pans, gets close to clean. So we are sorting out different problems according to different household trends around the world.'

In China, which is the third-largest market for Henkel behind the US and Germany, the situation is different again. Henkel found there was low penetration of dishwashers because for many middle-class households it was cheaper to employ a maid: 'Chinese consumers are not sensitive to household washing or laundry items, but they care highly about personal appearance. So, the pricing-point of personal care products relative to detergents is much higher than it is in Western Europe.'

Such international vagaries have persuaded Henkel to move more of its R&D closer to growth markets. Hence its research centre in Dubai has become a centre of excellence for laundry products that use less water. Its Asian R&D centres in China, South Korea and Japan are pioneering new hair-care and dye treatments.

Rorsted believes the industry is seeing a major innovation shift: 'What has changed in the process has been the globalisation of the innovation capability that we have. A lot of large companies, including ours, tended historically to have one or two major [R&D] sites and you would then take innovation from the West and move it to the East or the South. Now we have dramatically changed the footprint of where innovation takes place. So in five years' time, I am convinced that a lot more innovation will come out of China and out of Africa and the Middle East than in the last ten years.'

He denies categorically that part of the reason is cost, to reduce the overheads on R&D in lower-wage markets. He also rejects suggestions that Henkel products are becoming increasingly commoditised, with little price margin on its products.

Pointing to the example of Henkel's industrial adhesives business – its largest division by revenues – Rorsted argues there is significant margin upside from investing in innovation.

'If you take an iPhone, you simply cannot build an iPhone today without having sophisticated adhesive products. If you have a flat-screen television at home, you have adhesive between the different layers of glass.

'This adhesives business has come a long way since the First World War, when it was founded amid a German shortage of glues to stick boxes together. The division now serves industries from aerospace and automotives to consumer electronics and mobile telephony as well as packaging and building.

'There is tremendous innovation going on in adhesives. In electric cars, you can't weld carbon. That's all bonded together with adhesives. There is also innovation in aviation, in high and low temperature applications, in electronics and even in running shoes. The adhesive may be a low part of the end product price. But it's very technology intensive and very high margin.'

Whilst the return on investment in adhesives is derived increasingly from high-technology applications, pricing power in consumer products appears to be based on offering ever-greater household convenience. Innovation here seems to come from developing products that reduce the need for sorting clothes or rinsing dishes or mixing hair dyes. By making products easier to use, the company hopes its brands will gain a higher purchase consideration, thereby making its prices easier to defend.

If Henkel is on track with its strategy to globalise its operations, rationalise its brand portfolio and move innovation closer to end-user markets, the most significant challenge may be its goal to reduce market volatility and risk.

That risk was brought into sharp relief in 2014 when one of the company's detergent factories was destroyed in the Syrian civil war. Henkel's risk report, which runs to ten pages of its annual report, warned that 'continued unrest in Africa and the Middle East, in particular, could lead to rising material prices and supply shortages'. Rorsted does not know which side bombed the Syrian factory, saying simply, 'It's gone'.

Although losing a plant to civil war is extreme, Henkel faces other similarly unpredictable risks. With eight plants in Russia and six in Ukraine, it is exposed to the geo-political fault-lines of Eastern Europe. Rorsted is determined that Henkel will not withdraw from fast-growth markets due to unexpected international tension.

'We have been in Russia since 1991 and this has been the fourth crisis. So, strategically we are not changing our direction. Of course, tactically, what we do is we try and ensure that our people are taken care of;

that over time our assets are taken care of; that we mitigate some of the financial impact. But it doesn't change our view about where long-term growth is going to come from.'

Indeed, Henkel sees itself as a force for good in many of these more volatile territories. It says that it creates investment and jobs for local economies, manufacturing products that are more sustainable and better-produced than local alternatives, and that it treats its employees better than local businesses. It also claims to be serving national economies by creating indigenous centres of manufacturing, supply and demand.

Drawing a distinction with the clothing industry, which exports cheaply-made garments from low-wage to high-cost countries, Rorsted also adds: 'We have a different business model. Our business is not an export-driven business. We have plants in the regions where the products are being sold. If you take our Chinese plants, 90 per cent of them service the Chinese and surrounding markets. We make no exports from China to Europe; we have no exports from Bangladesh to Europe.'

The Henkel chief executive believes his model will enable the company to out-perform its competition as it continues to globalise and simplify its operations. He believes a strengthened global team, with more innovation outsourced to emerging markets, will inspire continued growth over the next five years. He maintains that long-term family ownership creates a timeframe in which to offset short-term risk, and to maintain its presence in markets where others fear volatility.

Laundry products, beauty care and adhesives may be unglamorous, increasingly price-competitive businesses to be in. But after more than 130 years of pursuing such growth, Rorsted says Henkel is determined to stay the course.

'We have benefited tremendously from loyalty and stability. The Russians or countries in the Middle East have seen that we have stuck around during periods when other companies might have pulled out. We just said we are in for the long term.

'This is central to the culture of Henkel. But it does require you to have a certain amount of ice in your stomach.'

Second opinion: the analysts' view

For an industry heavily exposed to consumer confidence and the slightest recessionary pressure, global consumer product companies are remarkably profitable. Operating margins at Henkel, Unilever, Colgate, Beiersdorf and L'Oréal are all comfortably in the mid-teens.

For each of them, the goal is to close the margin gap on industry leaders Reckitt Benckiser and Procter & Gamble, which boast margins of about 26 per cent and 20 per cent, respectively. But that job may be tough given cyclical and structural pressures on the sector in the years to 2020. The cyclical headwinds are linked to foreign exchange risks and the slowdown in Russia and Ukraine, which account for 8–10 per cent of revenues at Henkel. Its rivals are also spending heavily on promotions in the key US market, which could be a drag on margins. Any further slowdown in Europe, meanwhile, could lead to tougher competition from branded and private-label companies.

Structural challenges are harder to deal with. They include falling barriers to entry as technologies allow new brands to establish themselves online, and the arrival of what analysts at BTGI Research call the 'limitless aisle', where e-commerce enables consumers to search for almost anything from anywhere. BTGI warns that 'cost cutting is also likely to get more difficult as companies spend more to offset slowing growth and macro pressures'. Its analysts predict that Henkel may have to spend €2 billion on acquisitions to achieve its revenue target of €20 billion in 2016.

Henkel has two weapons in its armoury that should enable it, unlike some competitors, to make a calculated bet on revenue-enhancing deals. Those weapons are its adhesives business, where competition is limited and fragmented; and its controlling family-ownership, which has been supportive of the management's expansion plans.

The issue is whether the company can identify acquisition opportunities in adhesives that are not too expensive and that will continue to offset sluggish growth in laundry and homecare products. Given its ungeared balance sheet and divestments of lower growth brands, Henkel is certainly well placed to make a big move in advanced glues, for which demand is growing in the aerospace, automotive and mobile devices industries. The company also needs to expand in the Americas, where it is under-represented compared with P&G. The latter has a market capitalisation of more than $200 billion, compared with closer to $50 billion at Henkel.

Still, the German company has shown the industry the way by culling underperforming brands and investing in localised production. It enjoys a strong presence in emerging markets and has set itself demanding stretch targets for revenues. The key will be execution, and whether chief executive Kasper Rorsted can – like his detergents – transform dirty conditions into clean results.

Enrique Zambrano, Proeza

....

Annual revenues: $2.7 billion
Operating profit margin: c. 8%
Number of employees: 14,000
Country locations: 12 countries with manufacturing facilities
– Brazil, Argentina, Mexico, United States, United Kingdom,
Germany, Turkey, South Africa, India, Thailand, Australia, China
Headquarters: Monterrey, Nuevo León, Mexico

....

The chief executive of Mexico's leading automotive components
company and the country's largest citrus processing group has
led Grupo Proeza since 1988. He joined the family-owned
conglomerate after graduating from the Massachusetts Institute
of Technology and from Stanford, where he is a member of the
Advisory Council at the Graduate School of Business. In addition
to his role at Proeza, where he succeeded his father Guillermo
Zambrano, he is a board member at Alpek SAB, the Mexican
speciality chemicals and plastics group, and CFE, Mexico's
state-owned power utility. He is a member of the regional board
of Banco de México, and serves on the state board for the
Reconstruction of Nuevo León.

Rio Huichihuayan has little in common with the Rhine. One is bordered by orange groves and sub-tropical forests, interspersed with spectacular waterfalls in central Mexico. The other waterway carries more than 120 million tonnes of cargo annually from Europe's industrial heartland to the sea.

Enrique Zambrano values both. The chief executive of Proeza oversees an agro-industrial business harvesting thousands of hectares of citrus fruit in Mexico. He also has ultimate responsibility for a global automotive supplier, which includes several plants in North Rhine-Westphalia. Speaking at a riverside hotel in Cologne, after an overnight flight from Monterrey, Zambrano admits there is little synergy between processing citrus fruit and manufacturing chassis, engine cradles and fuel tanks for trucks, buses and cars:

'Our diversity is down to family entrepreneurship. It has been embedded for generations in a business that behaves like a portfolio manager,' he says. 'We try to apply lessons learned from one industry to another, and develop the sort of skills that are relevant to any business, such as finance and talent management.'

The Proeza story is a metaphor for Mexican industrialisation. In the mid-1950s, Guillermo Zambrano, Enrique's father, founded an engineering business, Metalsa, initially to produce metallic poles for streetlights. With help from some German engineering experts, it diversified into steel foundries. It even built a couple of ships. And in the early 1960s, Guillermo decided to invest in automotive components, forging an alliance with the US engineering group, AO Smith.

At about the same time, Mexico suffered unprecedented freezing winters that ravaged the orange crops. 'My grandfather had orange groves, and saw how quickly the fruit rotted in cold weather,' recalls the second-generation CEO. 'We knew industrial methods, and we thought there must be a way to save the fruit by processing it.' A sister company was thus formed alongside Metalsa: Citrofrut. Today, it is Mexico's leading processor of citrus and tropical fruits. Each year, the company processes more than 700,000 tonnes of citrus and other tropical fruits, supplying juices, oils and purées to global drinks groups and retailers.

Zambrano describes his father – who remains chairman of the Proeza board – as a visionary entrepreneur, who seized opportunities to build businesses that do not naturally sit together. In its latest diversification, Proeza decided to move into healthcare. It founded Zanitas, a provider of medical and hospital services that aims to improve community medicine, specialist services and emergency treatment in Mexico.

'This is part of our portfolio strategy,' explains Zambrano. 'Every six or seven years, we undertake a long-term plan that sets our goals for ten years into the future. At the last review, we said to ourselves: "We're in two capital-intensive and very cyclical businesses: automotives and fruit. What should we do to diversify and balance risk?" We went through several years of exploring healthcare as a new business area, before launching Zanitas in 2010. It's at an embryonic phase.'

The company plans to build new hospitals once it proves the basic business model, using each medical facility to test and adapt its health-care service. Yet even by 2020, it is expected to be a small part of the overall business, accounting for about 2 per cent of total revenues. Nevertheless, the vision to combine healthcare, citrus production and engineering makes Proeza one of the most diversified industrial groups in the world. Operating in a dozen countries with thirty manufacturing plants, with more than 7,000 hectares under cultivation and a growing network of medical centres, it defies the investment criteria of most institutional shareholders.

That is just as well. Because there are no institutional shareholders in Proeza.

'Proeza is totally family-owned. There have been no other share-holders in the parent group since its inception. It enables us to make decisions with a long-term strategic foundation. Public companies some-times have the pressure of quarterly results and their outside investors as their main driver. They also undergo frequent radical changes in strategy during leadership transition.'

Proeza has not changed strategy very often. The joint venture between Metalsa, Proeza's auto subsidiary, and AO Smith of the US lasted thirty-five years. When its Milwaukee-based partner sold its automotive division to Tower Automotive, another US components group, Proeza waited another ten years before taking back full ownership of the business. It then expanded Metalsa again in 2010 by acquiring the automotive structures arm of Dana, yet another US automotive components business which was restructured around that time. Two years later, Metalsa returned to the acquisition trail, purchasing ISE Automotive of Germany, which added ten manufacturing plants in Germany, China, South Africa, Turkey and the US.

Metalsa's formula – certainly with AO Smith and Tower Automotive – has been to identify distressed or underperforming yet fundamentally sound assets to buy, which debt-burdened parent groups may wish to sell. Having acquired them, it invests in product and technology, using advanced steels and composites, to broaden their customer appeal.

Each of these deals was financed internally by the Mexican parent company and credit facilities, without recourse to the stock market. According to Zambrano, the company learned its lesson in the 1980s.

'In 1982 and 83, the auto industry dropped by 60 per cent in Mexico and the peso devalued four times. It taught us to be low leverage and very careful in how to invest.

'During a crisis, banks lend only to the best credit-rated companies. If you have high leverage you lose credit-worthiness. In a sense we benefited from being prudent. In a crisis the best acquisition opportunities come along for those with cash and the balance sheet to take advantage.'

Today, Metalsa supplies structural components, chassis, hinges, transmission and safety systems to manufacturers from Bentley and Ferrari through to Skoda and Toyota. It has also dramatically increased its presence in Germany via relationships with BMW, Mercedes and VW, among others.

Metalsa's vision is to be indispensable to its manufacturing customers. As they move into new technologies or explore lower-emission engines, it has to be one step ahead. Zambrano says that is why it is working with advanced steels, composites and new manufacturing technologies that will help reduce weight and improve structural integrity in vehicles. Such investment has to be balanced against the cost of manufacturing in different countries. This involves a balancing act of being close to assembly plants in high-cost countries such as Germany whilst simultaneously evaluating the labour and logistics benefits of cheaper locations.

Zambrano predicts that by 2020 the group will have a network of plants in a mix of locations between highly developed economies and low-cost countries. This sort of balancing act does not apply to Metalsa alone. It is part of a wider balancing act in managing companies at different stages of maturity. Zambrano compares the varying maturity rates in business life to a family growing up: 'In our business, we have adults, youngsters and small children. Metalsa is mature and accounts for 90 per cent of the group. Citrofrut is a relative youngster, contributing almost 10 per cent of turnover, and Zanitas is the baby at about 1 per cent.'

The chief executive says the Zambrano family can afford to wait for each of these businesses to mature. And he is emphatic that Proeza does not need to list its shares or consider an initial public offering to fund further growth.

'To make an IPO you have to have size and liquidity. We are close to having critical size but we have no need for a listing. We have financed internally our acquisitions, and have a philosophy to reinvest most of the cash-flow in the business rather than pay out large dividends. It has been critically important that our shareholders are committed for the long term.'

Such long-term thinking is embedded across the company, nowhere more so than at Citrofrut, where the citrus groves have taken generations to establish. To deal with the produce, the company has opened three processing plants in the Mexican states of San Luis Potosí and Veracruz, a tropical fruit processing plant in Sinaloa, as well as a plant near São Paulo, Brazil, and a distribution centre in Texas. Processing remains close to the orchards because of the perishability of the raw material, although 90 per cent of the juice and by-products are exported around the world – primarily to the US, Europe and Japan.

Wholesale expansion in the Mexican fruit production and processing business has been constrained, nevertheless, by a land policy dating back to the 1930s. Back then, the Ejido system of government distribution of land to smallholders prevented the growth of large-scale industrial farming. There was some liberalisation of landholdings in the 1990s, when Citrofrut started acquiring cattle ranches and turning them into orchards, but most parts of the agricultural sector are not as productive as they might be.

This situation persuaded Proeza to harness some of its industrial manufacturing systems and philosophy from Metalsa and introduce them to an entirely different industry.

'We applied lean manufacturing processes and the sort of research and development approach from our automotive to our fruit business. This analytical approach helped us to improve yields in our orchards,' says Zambrano.

By improving yields, Citrofrut has been better able to match the domestic US producers, particularly in Florida where 90 per cent of production goes to processing. Its focus on pest and disease control has also helped win large processing contracts, particularly given the prevalence of 'huanglongbing' (HBL) or greening disease in Florida, which has contributed to lower US yields.

But a far larger competitive advantage may arise for Proeza from an unexpected quarter. It will not be about mechanisation or technology, but political reform. The 'Pacto por México', announced by President Peña Nieto, has been ratified by the country's three main political parties to push through a wide range of reforms. According to Zambrano, 'After many years without any major structural reforms – a period of low economic growth, increasing poverty and crime – we are seeing major policy changes that will be good for business.'

Since the cross-party reform pact was announced at the end of 2012, action has been taken to overhaul public education, liberalise telecommunications and open the state-owned energy market to competition. The reforms have not gone far enough to address wide wealth and economic disparities in Mexico. Nor have they addressed the vicious cycles of violence in some parts of the country, which prompted widespread protests in 2014. But business leaders believe the process is still a step in the right direction.

'There has been more constructive participation from the business community and society in general to put pressure on the government to modernise the country,' says Zambrano, who also sits on the regional board of the Banco de México. 'This internal transformation, coupled to an open economy, is enabling Mexico to become more competitive in advanced manufacturing including automotive, aerospace, white goods and electronics.'

He is particularly enthusiastic about the end to the energy monopoly of Pemex, the state oil group. A more diverse energy mix in Mexico could, he believes, herald the sort of shale-gas exploration that has transformed US utility costs. Zambrano explains that electricity costs in Mexico are more than 50 per cent higher than in the US. And he predicts that energy market reform will have tremendous competitive benefits for power-hungry businesses such as automotive manufacturing and agribusiness: 'In the US it has created a major benefit. There's been a rebirth of American manufacturing. Imagine what low-cost energy could do for Mexico.'

He sees an energy future for the country in which plentiful natural gas supplies form part of the utility mix, whilst incentives are introduced for renewable sources of power. If Mexico is ready to tackle powerful vested interests in energy, education and telecommunications, Proeza is hopeful the reform process could spread to the old Ejido system of land distribution. With greater opportunity to combine smallholdings, there would be opportunities to expand citrus, tropical and subtropical fruit cultivation in several regions where climate conditions are favourable.

'In the next three to five years, I think there will be some type of rural land reform. It won't mean that landowners in the Ejido system have to sell. But their small size is preventing them from being competitive, and the next generation of Ejido-owners have been moving to the cities. As they do so, we have an opportunity to rebuild the agricultural sector in Mexico.'

Zambrano insists this is not a precursor to a Proeza land-grab. Rather, it sees land reform as part of a package of measures to enhance local economies, with increased investment, job creation and financial returns for communities. Admitting that he gets too philosophical in explaining his business vision, Zambrano says:

'Making money or acquiring assets is a means, not the objective of what we're doing. Money is important, but it's the result of making the right business decisions and delivering a longer-term return to the communities in which we operate. It is not an end in itself.'

This approach is central to Proeza's system of values, which Zambrano says underpin what the company calls its 'humanistic-centric culture'. It partly explains Proeza's decision to diversify far away from its automotive and agro-industry roots – into healthcare.

'We have a mission to build a better community, creating economic and social value,' he argues. 'We are in twelve different countries and we have industrial capabilities, and we were looking for new opportunities. We were not about to go into gambling. We wanted to diversify into an area of less capital intensity, high-growth prospects and low cyclicality, which involved non-industrial assets and where we could leverage our philosophy and culture.'

After commissioning a study by Boston Consulting Group, Proeza has begun investing in community healthcare. Demand for higher quality healthcare is rising in Mexico, along with the means to pay for it. The group's Zanitas subsidiary aims primarily to serve the growing middle class in parts of Mexico where it has existing business activities. This demand is coinciding with a rise in medical problems common to more mature developed economies. An ageing population, changing diets, increasing obesity and related problems such as diabetes are all rising in Mexico.

'Using Proeza's skillset and philosophy, we think we can make an impact,' Zambrano claims. 'We want to deliver effective treatment techniques and drugs at affordable costs in smaller hospitals and community clinics. It is a very long-term exercise and part of a strategy that could take decades to deliver.'

The first Zanitas hospital has opened in Monterrey, offering services from short-stay surgery to maternity care, emergency rooms, specialist consulting and laboratory services. Initial plans to open a network of twenty hospitals have been scaled back, and Zambrano admits, 'We are still at the stage of defining the business model where we can grow as fast as we would like.'

Although Proeza does not disclose detailed financial figures, annual revenues of several billion dollars a year should generate sufficient cash to extend the new healthcare diversification. And the Zambrano family says it is extremely patient when it comes to returns. In calculating those returns and allocating investment capital, Proeza relies on a governance structure developed over the past fifteen years. Decision making by the group board reflects input from both shareholder representatives and external non-executive directors. Boards at each individual company agree their respective strategies, and seek approval from the Proeza board for major capital expenditure.

Zambrano says the disciplined governance structure also extends to deciding future family management, and who will participate in the future running of the company. Such decisions are shared with his brothers working in the group. The Zambranos regard filial ties as crucial in maintaining family unity, something which the chief executive says was drummed into them by their parents: 'Apart from maintaining a unified and committed group of shareholders, with each new generation there is a need to develop good board members. The need to be a good decision-maker as well as a good shareholder is fundamental to a family business, if it is to function properly and grow.'

He adds that there is no automatic right of accession within the family. Instead, the company is creating medium-term career plans for all executives, and identifying high-potential executives to deliver the strategy in 2020 and beyond: 'We are mapping in detail the talent we need to achieve our five-year plan; we are identifying where there are gaps; and we are bringing in some external executives that add very strong competencies in key areas.' By doing so, the Proeza CEO aims to build a business that will expand further through its Metalsa automotive business into the high-end passenger car segment. He intends to enter new developing markets around the world. And he has a vision to enhance healthcare provision in Mexico.

Zambrano's travel schedule reflects the breadth of Proeza's ambitions. After meeting with Metalsa in Cologne, his next stop is a healthcare centre in Poland. But first he must visit some of the automotive manufacturing plants in North Rhine-Westphalia – all within forty-eight hours of leaving Monterrey. He acknowledges: 'The businesses themselves don't fit together in any way in their day-to-day activities. But we bring value to them by transmitting our particular business philosophy and culture. Our legacy is about long-term thinking, management discipline and a humanistic approach.'

In the countdown to 2020, Enrique Zambrano predicts that Proeza's ability to deliver on that vision will be aided by structural reforms in Mexico, a strengthening economy and the growth of a better-educated workforce.

'Mexico might not be at the top in education,' says the MIT graduate running one of the country's emerging conglomerates. 'But the capacity to learn is amazing. We are entering a period of collaboration between government, business and unions that is getting stronger.

'This is dramatically different to what has gone before. It is our second revolution. It is the Mexican moment.'

Second opinion: the analysts' view

In the industrial and consumer supply chain, the producers of basic components or raw materials are the metaphorical canaries in the coalmine. Any production cutbacks among basic suppliers are a sure sign of caution elsewhere in the manufacturing sector, often triggered by waning confidence at the retail end of the chain.

That exposure is particularly true in two diverse industries served by Proeza: automotive and beverages. When deliveries and demand are on the rise, such companies flourish. When they falter, producers have to rely on cost-savings, pricing and inventory management to protect their margins.

Given the private ownership of Proeza, no analysts are making recommendations about the shareholder returns and growth prospects of the business. Instead, the fortunes of some of its largest customers are an indicator of likely demand. Taking Volkswagen and PepsiCo as two such customers, both are vowing to improve productivity and revenue management and introduce leaner operating models in the years to 2020. This will force suppliers such as Proeza to make similar adjustments.

VW has sent a cautious signal to suppliers by warning that GDP growth is behind forecasts in many of the markets it serves, and volume projections are likely to fall for the entire industry for the next several years excluding China, which is almost the sole growth driver for the industry. It is also asking suppliers to prepare for a world of shorter product lifecycles, more demand for sports utility vehicles, greater automation, tougher CO_2 regulations and economic uncertainty.

The German group is planning to make savings of €5 billion ($5.6 billion) on its core VW brand, including in procurement and seeking common parts. This will have implications for suppliers of body structures, safety systems, transmission modules, fuel tanks and other parts – all products made by Metalsa, the largest part of Proeza.

Similarly PepsiCo, the owner of juice brands Tropicana, Naked and Mirinda, is seeking savings in procurement and back office functions in order to protect margins in a deteriorating US beverages market. Analysts following PepsiCo see room to cut an additional $1.5 billion in costs if current savings plans do not materialise.

Such customer trends place the onus on suppliers such as Proeza's Metalsa and Citrofrut to make themselves part of the efficiency solution, rather than a high-cost problem. That means allocating more cashflow for reinvestment in new technologies and lower-cost production systems. Family-owned companies, with no external shareholders to please, can often increase spending or diversify into completely unrelated areas (such as healthcare, in Proeza's case) to offset near-term customer demands. That is one reason why Proeza invests more than 90 per cent of its cashflow back into the business. It is not a model that will lead to rapid returns for shareholders. But given those shareholders think in generations, not quarterly earnings, dynastic companies like Proeza have time to adapt.

Ashish J. Thakkar, Mara Group

Estimated net asset value: c. $100 million
Operating profit margin: Not disclosed
Number of employees: 8,000
Number of markets served: 21
Headquarters: Dubai

The founder of Mara Group and the Mara Foundation started his first IT company in 1996 in Uganda, when he was just fifteen. Mara Group has since emerged as an investment and industrial group with assets in IT services, manufacturing, real estate and agriculture. He is a board member at Mara Ison, a joint venture with Ison Group, an Indian IT services company operating in sub-Saharan Africa, as well as at Ison BPO, the business process outsourcing business that manages call centres, and at Riley Packaging, the East African cardboard packing group. Thakkar is also director of Atlas Mara, the pan-African financial services group that he co-founded with Bob Diamond, former chief executive of Barclays Bank. He also sits on the global agenda council on Africa at the World Economic Forum.

Appropriately, Ashish J. Thakkar wanted to meet at the Intercontinental Hotel in London. For when it comes to his business operations in twenty-two African countries, the founder of Mara Group regards himself as intercontinental.

Mara Group, launched in Uganda in the early 1990s, is one of a new generation of diversified pan-African conglomerates. It took its name from the region of Tanzania where Thakkar's mother was born. Mara also means lion in a Ugandan dialect, prompting the founder to adopt a lion's head as the company's logo. Eighteen years after its inception as an IT services business – importing parts from Dubai and reselling them in sub-Saharan Africa – Mara now spans real estate and property development, financial services, mobile technology, e-commerce, call centres, packaging and glass manufacturing.

In the most notable diversification from his technology roots, Thakkar joined forces in 2013 with Bob Diamond, the former chief executive of Barclays Bank, to launch Atlas Mara as a new African financial services group. Set up to rival established players such as Ecobank, United Bank of Africa and Standard Bank, it aims to shake up the financial services industry. Its vision is to pursue acquisition opportunities to expand across sub-Saharan Africa, offering access to capital and liquidity for commercial and retail operations in fast-growing African economies. Diamond, who stepped down from Barclays in 2011 following the Libor rate-setting controversy, is contributing experience gained building the UK bank's presence in Africa, where he also launched ABSA Capital, a pan-African corporate and investment bank, in 2005. Thakkar brings African operational experience together with governmental, regulatory and technology know-how to the venture.

In 2014, Atlas Mara took a step on its acquisition path with the takeover of BancABC, a mid-sized lender with operations in Botswana, Mozambique, Tanzania, Zambia and Zimbabwe. That was followed by the acquisition of the Development Bank of Rwanda as part of a government-privatisation programme. The deal coincided with events in Rwanda – attended by Thakkar and Diamond – to mark the twentieth anniversary of the country's bloody civil war. It was an emotional homecoming for Thakkar, who fled the genocide in Rwanda in 1994, returning two decades later as an inward investor and industrialist.

Born in Britain to parents who emigrated from Uganda in the 1970s to escape persecution of Asian communities, Thakkar had settled in Kigali, the Rwandan capital, just months before the genocide erupted.

'I was a refugee there. I saw what it was before and what it went through,' he recalls. 'It was fitting that the tag-line for the memorial events was "Remember, Unite and Renew".

'The economic renewal process followed a decision by President Kagame to send small teams to Singapore, where they spent ten days benchmarking and learning about its system. The difference between Rwanda and many other countries is that the delegations came back and started executing a reform programme. They have really created an innovative, investor-friendly and zero-bureaucracy business environment. Today, Rwanda is the Singapore of Africa.'

Thakkar dismisses suggestions that what is possible in a small country such as Rwanda may be hard to replicate in much larger economies such as Nigeria or Kenya. Instead, he maintains that the principles of strong corporate governance, an open economy, operational expertise and enhanced access to capital are relevant to the other forty-nine countries in sub-Saharan Africa. Still, he admits that there will be no one-size-fits-all solution in a continent that has been scarred by civil wars, natural disasters, corruption and generations of economic dislocation.

'I advise a few heads of state, some of them in East Africa, and the key to success is taking global business standards and adapting them to local market conditions. You can't replicate something that's worked in Uganda in Tanzania, or something that's worked in Kenya in Rwanda. You have to be local. And that's what we understand; we are local but we think African.'

Each of Mara's core business activities, which Thakkar describes as 'verticals', seeks to provide local expertise to commercial enterprises in different markets. It either builds from scratch or acts as the local partner to a large inward investor. At Atlas Mara, the thirty-three-year-old co-founder describes his role as active investor, contributor of technology and local-market adviser.

'We are not behaving like private equity shareholders, who know they need to exit at some point. Having a time bomb of needing to be out in five to seven years isn't the best way to build a really strong institution. We also decided against taking over a vehicle and trying to make it ours. We started from scratch.

'We have a blend that makes sense. It combines Bob's global financial services experience and passion for Africa, combined with my operational understanding of the continent in areas such as technology, mobile payment systems and as a business recipient of financial services in multiple different countries and companies over the last eighteen years.'

Atlas Mara believes there is a gap in the African market for new financial institutions following what it calls 'the retreat' of European lenders to their home territories following the sovereign debt crisis and tighter regulations on capital ratios. This exodus has created an opportunity for new entrants to provide much needed capital and liquidity for commercial borrowers engaged in building Africa's high-potential economies.

Mara Group is also engaged in building of a more physical kind through its real estate and property development business. That 'vertical' is involved in the construction of a new Intercontinental Hotel in Uganda along with a convention centre, shopping mall and office development. Mara is also a prime developer of two new hotels and shopping malls in Tanzania, and has finalised a joint venture with a luxury spa-hotel operator to open new resorts. At the same time, it is setting up a real estate investment trust, together with Standard Bank of South Africa, to co-develop and generate returns from greenfield and brownfield sites in southern Africa. The Mara founder is promising to 'change the face of our cities' with new building developments, focusing particularly on constructing shopping malls in cities away from the largest African capitals.

In the third business 'vertical' – technology services – Mara has expanded from a start-up selling computers, mother-boards and printers to distributing IT software and systems for social media platforms, instant messaging and mobile payments. The next step is the launch of an e-commerce platform, which Thakkar hopes will be an African rival to Amazon. Although he admits that sub-Saharan Africa's poor logistics infrastructure and low purchasing power make the rise of online retailing far from certain, he argues that Mara has the market knowledge and brand recognition to make it work if anyone can.

Alongside the three core businesses, Mara operates a family investment office that owns East and Central Africa's largest packaging manufacturer, the continent's first glass manufacturer and its largest independent call centre business. In each of the group's commercial activities, Thakkar characterises Mara as a disruptor to existing business practices, ready to move fast to seize new market opportunities.

That potential encouraged investors in London to subscribe in December 2013 to a public offering in Atlas Mara, which raised $325 million. In its presentation to potential investors, the new financial institution predicted that banks in the region could see a doubling of banking assets and deposits by 2020 as the growing middle class in sub-Saharan Africa starts to access financial services and commercial credit. Investors were also told that Atlas Mara had an opportunity to overhaul the African banking sector because there are a limited number of truly pan-African financial players.

As part of that disruption, Atlas Mara is pursuing selective bolt-on acquisitions and developing new financial services products targeting retail and small business customers. Some of those products will include new mobile payment systems, which have previously had limited penetration in many parts of Africa. 'Technology is also going to be massively disruptive,' Thakkar asserts.

'Being a social media platform and an e-commerce platform, with users with mobile wallets to plug into, is going to change the retail sector. The fact that somebody in a village can order something like you and me, and have a similar shopping experience to people in the West using online platforms – and then getting deliveries no matter how remote they are, is going to be a game-changer.'

His excitement is rooted in the potential growth profile of Africa, where there are more than fifty cities with populations exceeding a million people; where more than half the total population is expected to have discretionary spending power by 2020; and where GDP growth is forecast to out-pace most other parts of the world. Mara cites other indicators such as exploding mobile phone penetration, consumer spending that is expected to reach $1.4 trillion by 2020 and rising car sales, energy output and commercial air traffic, as reasons for optimism.

Thakkar acknowledges that sub-Saharan Africa still has major issues with corruption and other obstacles to doing business. But he says that regulatory conditions are improving and greater transparency is reducing the worst 'bureaucratic' issues of the past:

'Corruption is an important topic and there are a lot of issues in some of the countries where we operate. Mara has been working above board since it started and we brand everything Mara. We don't hide behind ten different names. But have we gone through bureaucracy? Of course we have. And the way we have managed it is to name and shame, and that's worked. In certain cases ministers have been fired. Because we now have a voice, because we're recognised, it's a lot easier to navigate.'

Mara's approach to addressing such issues has been to exploit its territorial knowledge and to behave as a local player in each market rather than a foreign inward investor. Its executives have gained that knowledge from supplying IT equipment to multiple nations since the mid-1990s.

'You have to really understand every single country, their history, politics, culture, their mind-set. That means operating in a local manner with global standards, and that's the basis for Mara's model.'

The rise of localism is seen by Mara as a natural evolution of African resistance to business colonialism or even regional super-powers such as South Africa seeking to exert their commercial influence on other countries. Thakkar says South Africa is learning from the mistake of saying 'get out of the way, you don't know what you're doing, let me show you how it's done'. He claims that some countries in East Africa now react adversely to South African commercial overtures and describes successful inward investors such as SAB Miller and Standard Bank as the exceptions. But he adds: 'There are pockets of opposition to South African businesses because of their historic sense of superiority. As a result, South African companies are becoming a lot more sensitive and aware that they need to be real partners in Africa. They are not the centre of gravity anymore.'

Nigeria, which in 2014 overtook South Africa as the continent's largest economy, has also tried and frequently failed to impose its way of doing business on neighbouring countries. The West African economic power-house, where Mara has more than 2,000 employees, also has significant problems of its own: dealing with the persistent threat of corruption and more recently terrorism linked to Islamic fundamentalism.

While acknowledging that such threats must be addressed, Thakkar says that Nigeria is continuing to make progress, and that the threats to business are more about perception and image than day-to-day operating challenges. Nevertheless, sub-Saharan Africa continues to face major structural challenges in sub-standard education, healthcare, sanitation and infrastructure – from Nigeria in the west to Ethiopia in the east, and including large parts of southern Africa.

Thakkar is passionate about the need for improved education and healthcare to raise basic living standards. But when it comes to commercial enterprise, he believes part of the solution depends on mentoring. In 2009, this led to the launch of the Mara Foundation, set up to provide comprehensive support services including business training, advice, start-up work-space, funding and mentoring for African entrepreneurs. The foundation now supports about 280,000 businesses in Uganda, Tanzania, Kenya, Nigeria and South Africa – with a particular focus on encouraging women entrepreneurs. Graca Machel, Nelson Mandela's widow, and Randi Zuckerberg, sister of the Facebook founder Mark Zuckerberg, are among the Mara Foundation ambassadors supporting this initiative.

With better advice, access to capital and mentoring, Thakkar claims that African small and medium-sized enterprises could leapfrog legacy European and American businesses. He says there is a huge opportunity in digital technology and mobile applications.

'Why can't the next Facebook, Twitter, LinkedIn, Uber – whatever – be innovated out of Africa? It is too narrow to just replicate global technologies that are invented elsewhere. We're not short of innovative ideas; we are short of execution. Instead of replicating what's already out there, let's do something that is going to be truly disruptive and fresh and exciting. We don't need to copy and paste anymore.'

He regards such a vision, however lofty it might be, as part of the long-term solution to Africa's economic volatility and structural challenges. To be successful, that solution cannot be delivered only in fast-growing economies such as Nigeria, Ghana or Tanzania. Behind the most progressive sub-Saharan economies, a second group of countries has been identified by Mara for investment. Tier-two countries – as Thakkar calls them – including Zimbabwe, the DRC (Democratic Republic of the Congo), Ethiopia, Mozambique, Mali and Malawi also need to embrace greater entrepreneurialism and business transparency if the continent's true potential is to be realised.

The Mara founder also wants the African Union to play a bigger role in removing impediments to cross-border trade and freedom of labour to ensure greater co-ordination of economic reform.

'I think the African Union's role is to ensure that progress happens at a similar pace and in a similar manner. But it's not happening fast enough. Take one example: it's easier for you as a British citizen to travel around our continent than it is for us Africans. It's ridiculous. Mobility and migration within Africa has to be better. Four African heads of state have signed a pledge to enable all African citizens to get visas on arrival in other countries. But where is the reciprocation? We need others to sign. The African Union should be naming and shaming them.'

Looking to 2020 and beyond, Thakkar's prescription for business in Africa rests on a combination of policy reform, improved business advisory services, greater access to capital, modern infrastructure and digital technologies that will enable economies to stimulate investment, job creation and growth. He sees Mara at the centre of that reform agenda, delivering improved access to capital and liquidity through Atlas Mara; new infrastructure through its real estate arm; and digital access through its technology businesses.

Thakkar is undaunted by the scale of the challenge. But he admits there is a metaphorical mountain to climb.

'I really think we are just getting started. There has never been so much global excitement around Africa. We may set up other verticals down the line as well. But it's just the beginning. For the last eighteen years, what we have been doing at Mara is laying the foundations – making sure we have the right execution capabilities, the right relationships, the right brand recognition and the right reputation.'

In the businesses where Mara is focusing its attention – banking, real estate and digital technology – the group founder says there are now tangible signs of strong progress. Tapping the Mara logo on his business card, he adds: 'The Indian tiger and the Chinese dragon have had their days. It's the turn of the African lion.'

Second opinion: the analysts' view

In the services industry there is no bigger geographic opportunity than that presented by sub-Saharan Africa. Arguably, there is also nowhere riskier.

Mara Group, and other diversified services companies investing in Africa, are betting that sub-Saharan GDP growth – averaging 5.4 per cent in 2014 – will continue to accelerate towards the end of the decade, bringing with it new investment in infrastructure, communications, financial services and manufacturing.

On the economic deficit side, many countries in the region continue to face socio-economic difficulties including disease, civil unrest, unemployment and shortages of food, foreign currency, manufactured goods and fuels. Infrastructure – a key barometer of progress – is under-funded in much of the continent, reflected in poor transport links and frequent outages in power and communications. On top of that, the legal system is risky for investors and companies.

Entrepreneurs such as Ashish Thakkar believe that the expansion opportunities far outweigh the challenges. He regards Africa as an 'exciting frontier market' for those businesses in which he invests. Analysts at Citi would seem to agree. They say that in the ten years to 2012, the services sector contributed more than 50 per cent of Africa's GDP growth. Demand for services is expected to grow as a result of urbanisation in more than fifty African cities with populations exceeding 1 million. The middle class, meanwhile, has expanded from 27 per cent of the population to more than a third in the first decade of the twenty-first century, according to the African Development Bank.

These trends are persuading Mara to expand in the business areas of IT, construction and financial services, where it is a founder and leading shareholder in Atlas Mara – the emerging pan-African banking group. The bet for Atlas Mara is that improving political stability, increased inward investment and demographic growth will enhance demand for domestic lending and commercial banking. It is also pinning its hopes on more regional integration in the sector. That is why Atlas Mara made three significant acquisitions in 2014.

In Nigeria, one of the markets where Atlas Mara is expanding, the business opportunity is clear from central bank statistics. They show that fewer than 30 million Nigerians have bank accounts out of a total population of 170 million.

For Mara Group, the basic strategy is to enhance efficiency and profitability in the services it provides, while improving risk management, introducing new products and pursuing growth in a way that overcomes sub-Saharan Africa's fundamental structural challenges. Its market opportunity may be enhanced by the reticence of other international players in terms of investment. As Atlas Mara said in its 2014 listing prospectus: 'There are significant gaps in the market today created by European financial institutions retreating to their home territories due to the sovereign debt crisis and the Basel III regulatory framework.'

If growth and stability continue to improve in sub-Saharan Africa in the coming years, the region could begin to close the gap – slowly – that exists between it and more mature economies. That will benefit the companies ready to exploit that shift. But it is a growth play based on considerable risk.

Linda Zecher, Houghton Mifflin Harcourt

Annual revenues: $1.38 billion
Operating profit margin: 24%
Number of employees: 3,400
Number of markets served: 150
Headquarters: Boston, MA
Imprints include: Education – Heinemann, Holt McDougal, Great Source, Rigby, Riverside, Saxon, Steck-Vaughan; Adult/General interest – Houghton Mifflin Harcourt, Mariner Books; Children – Houghton Mifflin Harcourt Books for Young Readers, Clarion

The former Microsoft executive became president and chief executive of Houghton Mifflin Harcourt in September 2011, with a mandate to turn the group into a global leader in educational content, with a growing digital presence. At Microsoft, from 2003–11, she led the corporation's $8-billion-a-year business serving government, education and healthcare clients in more than 100 countries. She previously worked at Texas Instruments, Bank of America, PeopleSoft, the human resources business, Oracle and Evolve Corp, the IT solutions business. The graduate of Ohio State University is a non-executive board member at Hasbro, the US toys and games group. She has served on several other boards, including the Intelligence National Security Association and the US State Department's Board of Overseas Schools.

The world's most popular ape is a chimpanzee called George. Since 1941, George has entertained millions of children with his infectious curiosity. He is rather good with crayons; he likes games. Most of all, George loves books. For more than seventy years, Curious George has also been the public face of a corporation. Some 75 million books about Curious George have been sold by Houghton Mifflin Harcourt (HMH), the US group that is one of the world's largest textbook publishers and providers of educational content. George is part of an enterprise that today reaches more than 50 million school-age children in over 150 countries.

The cartoon character is an important player in a global market for education, books, teaching materials and digital content that will be worth about $40 billion a year by 2018, according to forecasts by PricewaterhouseCoopers (PwC). By then, the schools market will have changed beyond all recognition from the one that George entered during the Second World War, when his character was first invented by German authors Margret and H. A. Rey. The online world has enabled George to fulfil a new vision to reach millions of new readers. He has a collection of digital properties and in 2014 he featured in an interactive story-building app *Curious About Me*, the latest in a series of Curious George apps designed especially for iPhone and iPad.

Linda Zecher, president and chief executive of HMH, believes that the animated chimpanzee is part of a revolution in educational content and distribution. 'Our industry in 2020 is going to be a software service model,' she claims. The former Microsoft executive, who joined HMH at the start of the 2011/12 academic year, adds: 'The future in education is going to be about content that's available anytime, anywhere. You are going to see a lot less education in bricks and mortar, or taught in the traditional way. And I think digital is going to allow that to change.'

Her vision heralds a potentially sweeping change for the education sector, where total spending on schooling equates to about 6 per cent of gross domestic product in the OECD (Organisation for Economic Co-operation and Development) group of industrialised countries. The growth opportunity is even greater in emerging markets, where an estimated 55 million children currently receive no formal education whatsoever in low- and middle-income countries, most of them in sub-Saharan Africa.

Zecher is targeting significant growth in international markets. But the content and distribution systems that could redefine education for generations of children are likely to be piloted first in the US, where HMH is based. In its home country, HMH commands more than 40 per cent of the market for educational books, digital content and teaching materials in the so-called 'K-12' segment: the age range from kindergarten to grade 12.

Achieving that market share has come at a price. In the spring of 2012, HMH filed for Chapter 11 bankruptcy protection after suffering from cuts in US education spending and the debt-servicing costs on more than $3 billion of borrowings. Those borrowings were amassed by the financiers who created HMH by first acquiring Houghton Mifflin in 2006, and subsequently Harcourt from Reed Elsevier of the UK. It was the culmination of a troubled period in which, over the course of a decade from 2001, Houghton Mifflin went through multiple restructurings and ownership changes, passing from the hands of Vivendi to various different private equity groups, before being forced into a major debt-for-equity swap in a court-supervised restructuring.

HMH emerged from bankruptcy with its borrowings dramatically reduced to approximately $250 million, all legacy debt eliminated and a new revolving line of credit to support future growth. The streamlined business, bolstered with senior managers whom Zecher recruited from her alma mater Microsoft, marked its revival with a stock market listing at the end of 2013. On its trading debut on the NASDAQ exchange, HMH's share price closed 30 per cent above the lower end of its IPO price range. The share price jump symbolised a cyclical and structural change in the company's fortunes. After several years of austerity in US state spending, there has been a general upswing in cyclical budget allocations to education. At the same time, education chiefs and governors in forty-five states have agreed to develop 'Common Core', a new K-12 standard curriculum for reading and mathematics. This has unlocked a huge demand for educational materials just as school authorities are digitising all aspects of learning.

'I think the inflection point is here,' says Zecher. 'We are benefiting from a combination of Common Core, pent-up demand in states that are flush with money, and school boards saying "Hey, wait a minute, if we're going to be buying new materials and doing teacher training, I want digital content." On top of that, you've got parents out there saying, "I don't want my child to get behind; let's give them digital content at home." So I think the transition to 2020 is going to be dramatic.'

The digitisation of US education is starting to reduce the cyclical nature of the old schoolbook adoption system. Previously, companies such as HMH in the US and UK-based Pearson did well when the populous states of California, Texas and Florida re-ordered books. When they weren't buying, publishers struggled. Now, every US state adopting the Common Core curriculum is buying digital materials. By doing so, they are hoping to bolster statewide education scores, which are seen as an important spur to wider investment, job prospects and wealth creation. Now digitisation is reducing the lumpiness of the renewal cycle because online materials can be refined and updated constantly, not waiting till the next print edition of a textbook.

HMH has responded by changing its entire development cycle, importing some processes from Microsoft where Zecher was in charge of its worldwide public sector business, including government, education and health.

'HMH used to have a print development team and a digital development team. They were different organisations producing different content,' she explains. 'We now develop everything digital first, and print becomes a distribution vehicle.'

When Texas ordered new K-12 maths materials in 2014, 70 per cent of the content supplied by HMH was digital. But not all states are so advanced, and print still accounts for more than half of all educational content across the US. The variable penetration of digital education is replicated outside the country. American schooling materials sold to South Korea and China are mainly digital, but in the Middle East most of the orders are still for books. Other markets, including South America, are buying hybrid materials: a combination of books and digital content. This has prompted HMH to bundle its content in print–digital packages, which Zecher says will allow different countries to pilot online content before transitioning schools from educational hardware to software. This graduated approach reflects one of the major challenges in the count-down to 2020: schoolchildren are proving more digitally literate than their teachers.

'My three-year-old grandson can pick up his iPad and find his stuff on it himself; when he sees a monitor, he thinks you should touch it,' Zecher recalls. 'Young digital students think differently and are wired differently. But the issue for teachers is not just generational, or whether they grew up with technology. Just giving an iPad to a child is not going to teach them Russian. Teachers have to learn how to leverage tech-nology. They have to know how to present it. So there is a part of the teaching discipline that needs to change in order for teachers to take full advantage of technology.'

The problem is exacerbated by the slow pace of change in colleges of education, where the fundamental way that teachers are trained has not caught up with advances in the classroom. As a result, educational publishers are now including technology training to support educators. More than 250,000 teachers attended HMH courses in the summer of 2014, where they learned how to use new digital materials to meet indi-vidual student needs and styles, and how to leverage online content rather than relying on out-of-date books.

The vision is that more advanced technology and more advanced teachers will, together, lift overall education standards. Teaching materials will become more interactive, with regular updates from materials stored in the cloud. Online materials could be automatically updated to reflect changes such as the re-designation of the planet Pluto, for example, or new scientific discoveries. Similar revisions could be applied to maps, dictionaries and other reference works.

'Instead of working to a six-to-seven-year adoption cycle, we can move to a maintenance type approach, where content is updated annually to make sure it's as fresh and robust as possible,' says Zecher. 'The benefit of technology is that your content is going to continually get smarter. As kids use it more and more, you can start using adaptive engines that allow teachers to understand why a student made this or that mistake. This leads to better learning outcomes for the child. This is a big change that we will continue to implement.'

Two other big changes are changing the nature of the K-12 education market: increased intervention by parents, particularly in pre-school learning, and growing internationalisation of teaching materials.

Companies such as HMH see a new opportunity in the 'pre-K' market, before children even attend kindergarten. An estimated $4 billion a year is spent in the US alone on home-educational products, with spending on children aged one to seven estimated at $240 per head, per year. Given that 60 per cent of American three year olds are not enrolled in any early childhood education, compared with an average of 30 per cent in other OECD countries, there is a huge target audience for pre-school sales. In the US, this is not seen as a problem; it's seen as a business opportunity. It is persuading educational content providers to expand their marketing campaigns from school and state authorities to stay-at-home parents and grandparents.

As part of this direct-to-consumer trend, in 2014 HMH launched an online 'Go Math Academy' that was targeted both at schools and parents. Zecher believes the penetration of such materials and a move to online subscriptions will, in her words, 'flatten the camel'. In time, it should reduce the schoolbook industry's dependence on the cyclical adoption patterns of large US states. For publishers, there is an additional benefit. A reduced reliance on printed works will lead to major savings in printing, warehousing and distribution.

But that vision is some way from full realisation. Even in America's digitally-advanced market, most states still rely on printed books for 70 per cent of their teaching materials. Larger states such as Texas might be adopting all-digital platforms for reading and maths, but the transition is proving slower in other subjects that are not yet part of the Common Core curriculum. Teachers, meanwhile, are taking time to adjust to online materials, and colleges are adapting relatively slowly to the digital era when it comes to teaching the teachers.

Given those challenges, it may not be until the first-graders of 2020 that we see the first generation to be educated without printed materials – at least in the US. Still, HMH is pressing ahead. The business case for doing so is clear: 'When you move to a digital model you have an opportunity for a significant amount of deferred revenue because it will be based on renewable subscriptions,' says Zecher. 'This more predictable revenue model also creates an opportunity for market expansion.'

Hence her digital vision sits alongside an ambition for international growth. Outside the US, Curious George is proving a helpful ambassador for that expansion. After the animated chimp launched his latest app, the highest downloads outside the US were in Australia, Japan and Saudi Arabia. The appeal of such materials, allied with rising demand for English-language learning, is turning Curious George and his fellow educational characters into an export asset.

'We think the international market is going to continue to grow, especially in places like China where a tremendous amount of money is going into pre-K learning now that they've relaxed the one-child rule,' says Zecher.

Her optimism reflects industry forecasts about potential demand in China. According to analysis by PwC, China overtook Japan in 2014 in terms of book demand, and is likely to overtake Germany in 2017. By the end of the decade, revenues in China are expected to exceed $13 billion, with educational and professional development expected to drive that rising demand.

However, few industry experts think this market opportunity is going to be left only to traditional educational companies such as HMH. Hundreds of new educational start-ups are targeting schools and purchasing authorities with alternative online models. Technology giants such as Google and Amazon are also expanding into education, whilst media groups News Corp and DMGT are building up their own educational businesses. So HMH faces a potential pincer movement that could drive down prices and threaten margins.

Zecher is unfazed. Under her leadership, HMH has become a predator of smaller rivals, acquiring several promising online players. Since its stock market listing in 2013, the group has purchased Choice Solutions, a US data analytics business in the education sector; SchoolChapters, an ePortfolio company dedicated to standards-based education quality management and accreditation services; Curiosityville, an online learning platform for three to eight year olds; and Channel One News, an online content provider for elementary, middle and high school pupils.

'The acquisitions we've made have been what I consider small tuck-ins, none have been significant large investments,' she says. 'They all allowed us to get further down the line faster and cheaper than if we built them ourselves. They also brought extra capabilities into the company, and extra talent that we didn't have as we made the transformation to digital.'

At the other end of the scale, she does not sense imminent danger from the technology giants of Silicon Valley. Instead, she envisages partnerships to marry HMH's content with the latest software emerging from such companies. HMH believes it has a fairly strong negotiating position with the technology players, because of the highly-regulated nature of educational purchasing and the strength of established publishing brands.

'We talk to Google and Amazon and Microsoft all the time. They have very large education organisations. But content is king, and teachers and administrators who are graded on the outcomes of students don't want to throw the baby out with the bathwater by abandoning trusted brands.

'There's a big barrier to entry in this market. So I'm not particularly concerned about being replaced because of the strength of our content and our relationships. But what I do believe is that we should be going in together. This is a journey in education, and technology can be such an enabler that it will be a great opportunity if we can get the partnerships right.'

Part of her confidence rests on concerns about data protection and privacy. Established publishers, endorsed by schools and colleges, are more likely to be trusted by parents and teachers as safe sources of materials and interactive learning compared with companies better known in relation to retailing or social networking. Publishers such as HMH and Pearson have also hedged against their exposure in the education market. Pearson has a strong media franchise in the shape of the *Financial Times*, along with a 50 per cent stake in *The Economist*, and a stake in the Penguin–Random House consumer book alliance. Boston-based HMH has expanded its consumer publishing arm in fiction, non-fiction and reference books, which offer an alternative revenue stream to its core business. Although education represents approximately 90 per cent of HMH revenues, Zecher says the group's rights to titles such as *Lord of the Rings*, *The Little Prince* and *The Hobbit*, along with ownership of imprints such as Wiley's culinary portfolio and *Webster's New World Dictionary* shows it has a strong future in consumer titles, too.

With such assets behind her, Zecher believes that she has the building blocks in place to deliver her long-term vision. That vision comprises improved profitability, international expansion, an investment shift from print to digital and more direct-to-consumer sales. And she sees these trends accelerating.

'The uptake on digital content is moving very rapidly. Do I think it will ever get to 100 per cent? No. You will always have children's books, and people still enjoy the concept of sitting on a bed with their child and reading a book.

'From an educational standpoint, the big challenge has been getting teachers prepared, getting teacher-training improved and more bandwidth in classrooms. But we could get to 80–90 per cent digital in education. We are ready; we prefer to sell digital content. It's better for the company; it's better for our ability to make updates and maintain content. And I think it's better for educational outcomes.'

Second opinion: the analysts' view

In global business, there are two product markets that are considered to be more or less recession-proof: nappies and coffins. Those sectors have a guaranteed customer base. A third is probably education.

No matter the economic cycle, governments, education authorities and ultimately parents want to educate children. That should be good news for producers of textbooks, teacher training and testing materials. Certainly companies such as Houghton Mifflin Harcourt (HMH) and Pearson do well when schoolbooks are updated in the core curriculums of English and mathematics. The entire sector is, for example, likely to benefit when California orders new reading materials in 2016.

Rising American demand is good for HMH. But it is not as international as Pearson, which means it is over-dependent on a home market where state spending is highly cyclical and where new technology companies could pose a competitive threat.

Like so many other sectors (but not yet nappies or coffins), education is being disrupted by digital technology. In some US states, notably Texas, entire parts of the school curriculum are moving from printed materials to digital content. On the plus side, digital content is cheaper to produce and easier to update. But on the downside, spending on digital content tends to be spread or even deferred over several years. And it involves significant upfront investment in the requisite technologies.

'HMH is highly reliant on state budgets and cyclical weakness could lead to deferred purchases,' according to analysts at Wells Fargo Securities. 'In addition, the market for K-12 materials is experiencing change and the desire for more digital content could create inroads for competitors and pressure on pricing.'

Education content companies are reacting by building hard-to-replicate digital franchises in particular subjects, offering multi-year content deals to state purchasing authorities that new entrants find hard to match. HMH is further protecting its business model by targeting parents and grandparents of pre-school children, hoping to win a loyal following who will expect to see the same branded teaching materials used in schools. Alongside that effort, it is seeking to internationalise its content and expand into teacher training, where there remains a consistent 'digital deficit' among staff trying to get to grips with technology. There is, nevertheless, a question about whether growth in those areas can compensate for any spending curbs on the traditional textbook adoption cycle.

Legacy competitors and new rivals, among them tech giants such as Google and Facebook, could pose a potential threat to HMH's leadership of the market for K-12 educational content. However, HMH should be able to defend both revenues and margins as long as it can embrace digital content fully and manage its costs in such a way to withstand pressure on school budgets.

That balancing act could, of course, make HMH a takeover target, particularly for technology companies seeking to increase their exposure to education or for established rivals seeking greater scale.

Bid activity aside, Trace Urdan at Wells Fargo predicts: 'HMH is well positioned, in our view, to benefit from a robust outlook for school spending over the next several years ... We expect the company to benefit as well from cost-savings resulting from the continuing migration of demand for digital content over print.'

Roberto Quarta, Smith & Nephew

Annual revenues: $6.69 billion
Operating profit margin: 18.6%
Number of employees: 14,000
Number of markets served: 100+
Headquarters: London

The American-Italian businessman is best known for his engineering skills – manufacturing and financial. He became chairman of Smith & Nephew in April 2014 after a career spent mainly in the automotive, aviation and specialist materials sector. From 1993–2001, he was chief executive of engineering group BBA Group and served as chairman from 2001–06. Quarta transformed the former British Belting & Asbestos into a world leader in vehicle systems and aviation services. He is also former chairman of Rexel, the French electrical supplies company, and a former board director at BTR and BAE Systems. In 2015 he will become non-executive chairman of WPP, the advertising and marketing group, and will stand down as chairman of IMI, the FTSE 100 engineering business. Quarta remains chairman of the European arm of Clayton Dubilier & Rice, the private equity firm.

Most patients undergoing hip replacements or knee surgery would expect a surgeon or two, an anaesthetist and several nurses in the operating theatre. They might be surprised to find a representative from a medical device company in attendance.

Smith & Nephew, however, one of the world's leading medical technology companies, does not merely supply orthopaedic joints. It also supplies specialist representatives, who are available to assist the surgeon with implant sizing and to ensure the correct surgical instruments are available. The company officials never touch the patient or intervene in the operation itself. They are there to ensure that exactly the right implant or instruments are used from a number they may have ready for the procedure. Their presence is a long-standing tradition – and a significant expense – in the $14 billion industry for hip and knee implants.

It is part of a broader change in healthcare, in which companies providing all manner of medical services and treatments are adapting to fast-moving socio-economic trends. This industry is undergoing a major reorganisation amid widespread budgetary pressures on hospitals and healthcare providers. The transformation in healthcare purchasing reflects both the challenges posed by ageing populations and the prevalence of obesity, and the opportunities created by new technologies, the desire for a more active lifestyle, biological therapies, new implant materials and data management.

Smith & Nephew is one of the global 'med-tech' companies adapting to an upheaval in medical budgets, technology and treatment procedures – not just in hip and knee implants but in every segment that it serves, which includes the $6.7 billion market for advanced wound management, the $4.9 billion market for trauma and 'extremities' and the relatively fast-growing field of sports medicine, worth an estimated $4.6 billion per year.

Roberto Quarta, chairman of the British company, says: 'Our whole industry is trying to focus on the total cost of care. In a market where less money has been spent on healthcare in real terms since the financial crisis, and where product prices are under pressure, and where technology and the latest advances can promise better patient outcomes, it's clear that we have to rethink the business model.'

The latest market transformation follows a history in the healthcare industry of fundamental and repeated restructuring, dating back to when Thomas James Smith founded the company bearing his name more than 150 years ago. A business that began by supplying bandages now produces silver-coated antimicrobial wound dressings, cementless hip systems and knee implants that are lab-tested to simulate thirty years of wear. Its products include a host of other advanced medical devices such as bio-composite suture anchors for repairing shoulders, implants and instruments for reconstructing cruciate ligaments, variable-angle locking, low-profile plating systems for complex fractures, and plasma wands that use radio frequency to gently remove tissue.

The business, which generates around 40 per cent of its revenues in the US and a further 40 per cent in other mature industrialised economies, has emerged as a leading indicator of healthcare spending, particularly on devices, implants and wound management. The strategic vision of companies such as Smith & Nephew is being reshaped by three key factors: changing demographic trends; the rise of middle-class patients in emerging markets with an ability to pay for care; and increasing hospital investment in some of those emerging markets. They are considering how to adapt to a market defined by ageing populations requiring complex procedures, a growing proportion of them in emerging markets such as China and Brazil, where the middle class has an increased willingness to pay for elective surgery.

This is coinciding with greater spending on healthcare infrastructure in the developing world. In China, for example, more than $2.5 billion was spent on building or improving hospitals in mid- to smaller-size cities between 2009 and 2011, a significant increase on recent years.

Emerging market demand for reconstructive surgery and advanced wound management is now closing the healthcare gap between the developing world and more advanced mature economies. Overall patient need in both developing and mature markets is also expected to rise, given the global trends of ageing populations and chronic long-term medical conditions. The number of people aged over sixty-five is expected to reach almost 1.5 billion by 2050 – a period in which problems such as obesity are likely to put a further strain on health-care systems. Research by consultants at McKinsey estimates that, of the world's 7.2 billion inhabitants, more than 2 billion were classed as obese in 2013, representing a 28 per cent rise among adults and a staggering 47 per cent jump among children compared with the figures in 1973. That, in turn, is leading to a rise in the incidence of diabetes, affecting almost 390 million people worldwide, according to 2014 estimates by the International Diabetes Foundation.

At Smith & Nephew, Quarta is alarmed by the societal impact of such trends. But he sees a market opportunity when it comes to treating conditions linked to obesity, diabetes and ageing. It should drive up the numbers requiring joint reconstruction with devices or implants supplied by companies like his. The chairman also sees an upside to changing lifestyles and an improving global economy.

'More people are wearing out their knees and hips than they used to, due to living longer, more active lifestyles and, conversely, greater obesity,' he explains. 'In the developed world the rate of growth in replacement hips and knees has been proportionate to the Baby Boom generation hitting their sixties and seventies. This generation is more active and therefore more likely to need orthopaedic repair or replace-ment. That slowed down during the recession, because if your surgery wasn't totally covered by insurance or if state healthcare budgets were stretched, then elective operations were put off. Now we're seeing a pick up because the economy is improving and surgery is becoming more accessible again.'

An improving outlook, however, could be threatened by the grow-ing influence of procurement departments in healthcare. Cash-strapped health authorities are striving to drive down product purchasing costs. Quarta, who is also chairman of the British engineering group IMI, sees a worrying parallel with another sector in relation to cost-cutting on medical device spending.

'It's a bit like the auto industry, where a car-maker might buy a cheaper casting because it should fit the spec, but once it's machined it takes twenty minutes longer and might require adjustments. But the purchasing guy is only looking at the material cost. It's the same with medical devices: a higher spec product might allow the patient to get out of hospital sooner, enjoy a better outcome and reduce the need for repeat surgery, and thus result in savings on the overall healthcare cost.'

As a result of pricing pressures and healthcare budgetary constraints, the rate of growth in the hip and knee replacement market has shrunk to 3–4 per cent a year, down from double-digit growth a decade ago. Smith & Nephew's response has been to rebalance towards higher-growth segments, investing in sports medicine and trauma and extremities. In the second quarter of 2014, for example, the company enjoyed 9 per cent revenue growth in sports medicine joint repair compared with 2 per cent for knees and 3 per cent for hips. Sports medicine joint repair is one of seven higher-growth segments in which the company is expanding.

'At one end of the spectrum, it caters to younger people who regularly play sports,' says Quarta. 'What you see on television is wonderful, but for every extraordinary performance there are many more who are hurt in the process. At the Winter Olympics or world championships, you see all these people on snowboards doing tricks; many of them have lots of pins, anchors and plates – that's sports medicine.'

The field of sports medicine has flourished thanks to the rise of middle-aged 'weekend warriors', usually men who are surprised at their skeletal frailty. The rising incidence of sporting accidents from bikes, climbing, skiing and a range of activities deemed higher risk by the insurance industry is good news for companies that are delivering pioneering medical advances. Many more of the sporting injured are electing for restorative surgery rather than living with degenerative joint conditions.

Off the sports field, Smith & Nephew is forecasting promising growth in emerging markets, in trauma and extremities (wrists and ankles), gynaecology, advanced wound bioactives and advanced wound devices. Of those areas, the UK group expects that a quarter of its revenues will come from emerging markets by 2020, up from 13 per cent in 2013. Quarta says the challenge in emerging markets, both for reconstructive implants and wound care, is one of affordability. In India 60 per cent of healthcare expenditure is paid out-of-pocket, and in China around 40 per cent. As a result, the volume of reconstructive surgery undertaken in China is only a quarter of that in the US. But demand is expected to surge given that China's elderly population is more than twice that of America. In his words: 'We are working on developing knees and hips that deliver the same quality but at a different value point, providing relief and improving the quality of life for people in those markets.'

The company has also strengthened its ethical and compliance standards, with policies, training and controls in place to govern all interactions with healthcare professionals and for activities involving third parties such as distributors in emerging markets. All medical technology companies have put in place strict guidelines on how they market products to healthcare purchasers. Controversial sales practices in the pharmaceutical sector – including accusations of corruption involving drug companies seeking preferential orders in markets such as China – have led to a clampdown on the use of sales agents and other incentive-based sales techniques.

Aside from expanding its presence in emerging markets, Smith & Nephew is focusing on two visionary concepts: dramatic advances in wound management and greater automation in its 'point-of-care' services in the implant market.

Specialist wound care is expected to be a major growth area given the incidence of conditions that demand sophisticated wound treatment. Citing figures that show 48 per cent of all venous leg ulcers re-occur within five years, Smith & Nephew is investing in advanced therapies and dressings. The company that supplied bandages for the wounded in two world wars is now developing dressings that automatically measure the health of a wound and relay data to nurses. It is also offering 'negative pressure' wound therapy.

Such advanced devices are being applied alongside 'bioactives', an area growing at about 15 per cent a year. Instead of cleaning wounds with saline and a scalpel to remove dead tissue, the next-generation care system uses enzymes to eat dead tissue and enable healthy flesh to repair itself.

'Wound care is jumping ahead of orthopaedics in terms of evolution, both in products and solutions for patients who have the most horrible wounds you can imagine,' argues Quarta. 'We can now treat, reduce infection and help the wound to heal faster and thereby reduce pain and suffering. When you see these people with 90 per cent burns or soldiers who come back from war zones with terrible injuries caused by improvised explosive devices, bombs and shrapnel, you can understand why this is an important area for us.'

He claims the company's emphasis on advanced wound care – a segment in which it competes with rivals such as Molnlycke, Acelity and Convatec – coincides with changing healthcare provision in industrialised markets:

'The sophistication of the products has moved forward at a faster rate than the medical profession's skill-base in treating wounds. So what was traditionally done by a GP, who knew how to sterilise and apply a bandage, or in the Emergency Room, is leading to a whole new industry of specialist wound care facilities in the US.'

New specialist facilities have opened following a realisation among US healthcare providers that they were lagging behind Europe in advanced wound technology. Tissue-viability nurses, for example, have become an important part of wound-care management in Europe, where centralised state procurement programmes ensured more sustained funding for such roles.

'But if you go to emerging markets you still see huge amounts of tapes and gauzes being used. Our challenge is to deliver the same quality at the same margin point to markets where affordability is a systemic issue,' says Quarta.

His vision requires a solution to the problem of affordability, where market demand and patient need are not always matched by the funding necessary to guarantee the best care. This is forcing a rethink of the overheads in the med-tech industry, not only in wound management but also in reconstruction. One of the largest costs associated with reconstruction remains the presence of company representatives in operating theatres, which has been a key part of the service for years. The cost of training and equipping such representatives is a major factor in reducing Smith & Nephew's gross margins from more than 70 per cent to a more modest, but still respectable, net 23 per cent.

In a bid to generate more attractive economics for patient, payer and healthcare provider alike, but without compromising clinical quality, in 2014 the group unveiled the 'Syncera' solution: an automated system to replace representatives attending surgery with a cloud-based model to manage supply chains, check joint size, improve inventories, provide online technical support and ensure the availability of replenishment implants. In future, surgeons will upload their requirements, scan the implants they are going to use and conduct video conferences from the operating theatre to discuss procedures – rather than consult with a company representative in person.

Smith & Nephew initially launched Syncera in the US, and expects it to be rolled out in Europe thereafter. By reducing waste and standardising its systems, Syncera aims to deliver significant cash savings of more than $4 million per hospital – based on 700 total hip and knee implant procedures over three years. This type of innovation is vital if med-tech companies are to defend their margins. Quarta is clear about the task facing the management team led by chief executive Olivier Bohuon, who joined the company in 2011, having previously headed a division of pharmaceutical group, Abbott. He has encouraged Bohuon to press ahead with the strategy to rebalance Smith & Nephew towards its higher-growth markets.

Their strategy includes delivering products that improve patient outcomes and access, whilst reducing the economic burden on healthcare systems, investing more in R&D and driving innovation into business models, such as Syncera, which promise new ways to serve customers. Product innovation alone, however, will not guarantee enhanced profits until such systems are widely accepted in the market. So investment innovation has been coupled to a search for savings elsewhere. In 2011, Smith & Nephew announced plans to generate annual savings of $150 million, and in 2014 launched a further programme to cut costs by at least another $120 million. Alongside innovation-spending and a far-reaching savings programme, the company has sought further scale through acquisitions.

In 2012–14, such reinvestment saw Smith & Nephew undertake thirteen acquisitions to expand its presence in emerging markets as well as into new treatment areas. They included the 2014 acquisition of ArthroCare, the US sports medicine company, for $1.7 billion. It brought with it technologies in minimally-invasive procedures and a leading position in shoulder-repair systems to complement Smith & Nephew's position in knees.

The chairman believes such 'bolt-on' (sic) acquisitions will strengthen the group's ability to offset pricing pressures in lower-growth parts of its business, whilst continuing to explore new business models, expand in emerging markets and bring the overall cost of healthcare down. Realising this vision, however, could prove every bit as complex as the reconstructive operations for which Smith & Nephew supplies the implants and dressings.

'In healthcare, we are part of the solution – not the problem,' Quarta claims. 'Buying the cheapest product can end up inflating the overall cost of care. We believe our products and market expertise enable healthcare professionals to heal more patients, faster, freeing up beds, and reducing the chances of coming back for further treatment. That's the ultimate goal.'

Second opinion: the analysts' view

The global market for medical technology, implants and wound management is expected to continue to rise. But the number of suppliers may shrink.

Equity analysts predict that pressure on costs and the expense of new technology will force consolidation among players such as Smith & Nephew. But the sector followers are divided on whether it will be predator or prey. Ian Douglas-Pennant at UBS says:

'We see a high likelihood that Smith & Nephew will be acquired. Scale appears to be increasingly important in the orthopaedic space, and even some of Smith & Nephew's own actions appear to point to a tacit admission that it needs to build scale; it bought Arthrocare to widen the breadth of its offering and is shifting investment away from hips and knees in developed markets.'

Alexander Kleban at Barclays, however, sees potential for the group to be the consolidator.

'It remains committed to pursuing deals when the fit is right,' he tells investors. 'This could imply multiple bolt-on acquisitions in parallel, provided this does not overload any of the businesses.'

Smith & Nephew's attraction – either as buyer or seller of assets – rests on its presence in higher-growth emerging markets for hip and knee implants, its greater investment in sports medicine and the development of clever proprietary technologies in negative pressure wound therapies. In those market segments, demand for wound care and related devices have slowed and prices have come under pressure in developed markets, such as Europe. This has been offset partly by strong growth in sports medicine.

UBS sees med-tech rival Stryker as the most likely suitor for Smith & Nephew. But it warns that the British company needs to manage a range of risks including, 'potential product recalls and product liability litigation, ensuring sufficient product development and approval, and healthcare expenditure trends. While generally S&N's markets are not fast-moving and customer loyalty is high, the company must keep up with trends in areas such as computer-aided surgery, unicondylar (or total) knee replacement, minimally-invasive surgery and biologics in order to maintain growth and grow market share.'

Given those risks, the company is expected to emerge by 2020 with a greater focus on wound management and sports medicine compared with its previous reliance on implants, whether as a standalone entity or part of a wider group. The market for wound care, which has been affected by budgetary pressures, is expected to stabilise, although pricing for hip and knee implants is likely to remain under pressure.

If Smith & Nephew can successfully navigate these market conditions, analysts predict that its revenues could jump from the £4.35 billion

($6.52 billion) announced in 2013 to £5.43 billion ($8.14 billion) in 2018, with net earnings rising from £694 million ($1.04 billion) to £1.1 billion ($1.6 billion) over the same period. Such a performance would represent a return to healthy financial growth for the business. But a potential acquirer may want to pounce before Smith & Nephew has a chance to prove its standalone fitness.

Martha Lane Fox, Go ON UK

....

Annual revenues: $1.9 million
Operating profit margin: N/A
Number of employees: N/A
Number of markets served: UK
Headquarters: London

....

One of the youngest members of the House of Lords, Lane Fox
sees her role as extending digital literacy, whilst holding
governments to account over digital surveillance. She chairs
the UK's public–private sector partnership aimed at improving
access to Internet communications. Lane Fox was a co-founder
of lastminute.com, Europe's largest travel and leisure website,
which was listed in 2000 and sold to trade buyers in 2005. Since
then, she has been appointed a non-executive director of Marks
& Spencer, the UK retailer, and in March 2014 was appointed
chancellor of the Open University. She is the chair of two online
companies: LuckyVoice, which claims to revolutionise the karaoke
industry, and MakieLab, the games and toys business. Lane Fox is
the former digital champion for the UK government.

In 1989, a British software engineer at CERN, the European Organization for Nuclear Research, drafted a paper called 'Information Management: A Proposal'. The paper proved to be the blueprint for the Internet. Tim Berners-Lee, its author, was later hailed as the father of the World Wide Web.

Since then, the Internet has transformed communications across the industrialised world, becoming indispensable for social and workplace interaction for an estimated 2.7 billion users – almost 40 per cent of the global population. In 2014, when Berners-Lee celebrated the twenty-fifth anniversary of his blueprint, he joined forces with other Internet entrepreneurs to extol a new vision 'to defend, claim and change the future of the Web'. The entrepreneurs calling for a strategic rethink included Baroness Martha Lane Fox, co-founder of lastminute.com – Europe's largest travel and leisure website – and chair of Go ON UK, a public–private sector alliance aimed at promoting online engagement. Together, Berners-Lee and Lane Fox are backing the Web We Want campaign, aiming to unlock the opportunities and freedoms first envisioned by dotcom pioneers at the end of the twentieth century.

'What has become clear is that the promise of 1997–98, when we started our business, has not yet been realised,' says Lane Fox, a former digital adviser to the UK government and now chancellor of the Open University. 'I never imagined that we would see so quickly a lock down of the Internet in platform terms.'

She acknowledges that the Internet economy is hugely valuable, helping to transform communications for billions of people. If it was a national economy, the Internet would rank the fifth-largest in the world behind the US, China, Japan and India in global value. By 2016, this Internet economy is expected to be worth $4.2 trillion as online retail, advertising, procurement and e-commerce gathers pace, according to forecasts by advisors BCG.

But Lane Fox, who also chairs two online start-ups, LuckyVoice and MakieLab, is worried. Rather than foster new enterprise, an open marketplace for commerce and social value, she fears the Internet has been captured by a hegemony of over-mighty corporations, on one hand, and, on the other, governments that appear to value data-collection above providing universal access and digital skills.

'It has become extremely tough to make it online unless you have a relationship with one of the big guns like Google, Alibaba, Apple, Facebook and Amazon,' she says. 'And then governments are not doing enough on the other side. They are not delivering full access fast enough, whilst alienating those that do have access because of data-scrutiny. The net result, I think, is the real danger that we will disenfranchise or leave behind a huge number of people.'

Internet evangelists point to the huge take-up of online technologies. They point to the estimated 1.8 billion photos shared daily, the 2 billion smartphones in use and the combined market capitalisation of Apple, Google, Facebook, LinkedIn and Twitter, which reached almost $1.2 trillion in 2014. Internet usage could reach 6 billion by 2020, according to the Ericsson Mobility Report, published annually by the Swedish telecommunications group.

Lane Fox is not so sure. Whilst applauding penetration of 2.7 billion halfway through the second decade of the twenty-first century, she adds: 'There are still more than 4 billion [people] who aren't connected. I am not sure about the techno-utopian vision that implies there is an inevitability that the whole world will be connected.'

She cites research by McKinsey, the strategic consultants, which warns of slowing growth in online usage. It identified five key drivers of Internet growth in the ten years to 2014, when an estimated 1.8 billion people joined the online community. That expansion was driven by rising mobile network coverage, increasing wireless-broadband adoption, urbanisation, falling device and data-plan prices, a growing middle class and the increasing utility of the Internet. According to McKinsey, 'Without a significant change in technology, in income growth or the economics of access, or policies to spur Internet adoption, the rate of growth will continue to slow. The demographic profile and context of the offline population makes it unlikely that these individuals will come online solely as a result of the trends that have driven adoption over the past decade.'

Part of the problem is that the easy-to-reach online markets are already well penetrated. And it is in these developed economies where corporations can secure revenues, subscribers and advertising that delivers a return on investment. The offline population, by comparison, is concentrated mainly in under-developed and primarily rural economies, where there is a lack of basic education and healthcare. If you don't have access to water or electricity, a Facebook page is not going to change your life.

But the barriers created by low incomes, poor user capability and absent infrastructure are not confined merely to parts of sub-Saharan Africa and the Indian sub-continent. Even in 2015, more than 10 per cent of the US population is expected to remain offline, with similar percentages in parts of Western Europe.

Lane Fox regards this as an indictment of government failures to embrace digital technologies with the same enthusiasm as private enterprise.

'We've got to be realistic that when you look back at what has been created over the last twenty-five years, a small number of people got a lot richer; some incredible business models have been created; amazing companies have been built employing many thousands of people,' she says. 'But it's not as though public health or public education has been transformed, or that we as individuals have suddenly been empowered and unleashed, and that a whole wave of creativity has been set free.'

Lane Fox's concerns are echoed at the European Commission, which fears a widening technology gap between the US and Europe, and a lack of digital engagement in many member states. Commission President Jean-Claude Juncker has vowed to accelerate the creation of a digital single market, hoping to break down national silos in everything from data protection legislation to the management of mobile spectrum.

He has also charged Günther Oettinger, the Commissioner for Digital Economy and Society, with ensuring more incentives for European technology research, support for start-ups and stimulating investment in cloud, big data and machine-to-machine communications. Oettinger's mandate includes the need to make Europe a leader in cyber-security preparedness and 'trustworthy ICT'.

All laudable goals, but analysts question how much will actually be achieved. One Brussels-based commentator says: 'No one knows how Europe will close the technology divide with the US and increasingly China. It all depends on what your definition is of the "Digital Single Market". If it is harassing technology companies about their use of private data and regulating Google, the Germans seem hell-bent on getting something done on that front. If it means actually creating a seamless market for all digital communications and transactions, don't hold your breath. The Commission has too much else going on to make this an absolute priority.'

Oettinger, a German politician and member of the Christian Democratic Union (CDU), nevertheless shows every sign of endorsing Lane Fox's determination to democratise the Internet. He has vowed to consider a tax on US companies such as Google to help fund the creation of a digital single market. And he has promised to explore new rules that would give online users greater protection over how their data is used by companies such as the US social media giants. Like Lane Fox, he wants to combine such protections with programmes to enhance digital literacy.

Just as in the UK, however, there is a gap between ambition and practical reality. And it seems clear that European efforts to ensure basic universal connectivity; to address perceived American dominance in search, e-commerce and social media; and to offer reassurance on data protection look rather defensive. Europe's approach contrasts with accelerating digital innovation in the research labs of the US and China. Only wrangling in the US over network management regulations for the Internet – the issue of net neutrality – poses any sort of obstacle to new forms of American content consumption or online distribution. In China, only the 'Great Firewall', enshrining state censorship of the Internet, has put a brake on the emancipating potential of new technology.

So geographically the technology sector appears to be a three-speed engine: high-gear growth in the US; solid expansion in China to serve its huge domestic audience; and a European model stuck between low-gear and neutral. This is not exactly what technology evangelists had hoped for by 2015.

In terms of fulfilling the Internet's potential, Lane Fox argues that the world is still at the beta stage – experimenting with new models, having already established that returns can be made from online search, social and e-commerce platforms. Such experimentation is not underway at technology companies alone. It is affecting every part of the corporate world, from financial services and manufacturing to retailing.

Lane Fox is well aware of the challenges, given her role as a non-executive board member at Marks & Spencer. She says that M&S has become one of the few British companies to elevate a digital executive to the main board: Laura Wade-Gery, executive director of the retailer's multi-channel business.

'That's a great start and a brilliant symbol,' she points out. 'But it's a big old organisation that is quite like the civil service, a national institution in the UK. They know they need to do it. But it's still hard.'

Whether you look at M&S or online platforms such as Google and Facebook, their consumer reach remains constrained ultimately by the sizeable portion of the global population that remains offline. After twenty-five years, universal Internet access still has not been achieved even in the most highly-penetrated online markets. This is creating a further barrier to next-generation online delivery. Services cannot be moved fully online, especially in health and education, unless an entire population is connected and able to receive them. And this exposes a fundamental problem: even if all households and all mobile users are able to access the web with secure superfast connections, that does not translate automatically into digital literacy and engagement.

As chair of Go ON UK, Lane Fox marshals a group of business leaders to address this challenge. They include the chief executives of retailer Argos, energy group E.on, the Post Office, and mobile networks TalkTalk and EE, along with the director-general of the BBC, the Big Lottery Fund and Age UK. Her priority is to encourage the government and private enterprise to deliver a universal high-quality online infrastructure and basic digital skills for all users.

Without those building blocks, the UK or other mature economies may not foster the number of digital start-ups or the sort of public services that will move the Internet from being a social and e-commerce platform to a basic utility that embeds technology in every part of society.

So Lane Fox believes government should intervene to subsidise universal broadband access and skills training: 'There are two top priorities: infrastructure must be improved. There are too many areas of the country where super-fast access is non-existent or inconsistent. In London, despite our mayor's claims, the infrastructure is pretty shitty. But that's just one part of the puzzle. The other half is about digital skills.

'That's why Go ON UK focuses on the 10 million adults in the UK who cannot do four basic things online: send an email, make a transaction, communicate safely and search. You can put as many fast connections as you like right under their door, but that's going to be irrelevant unless you train and educate people in the basics and explain why it might be helpful in terms of saving money, or education, starting a business or getting into work again.'

The willingness of the unconnected to embrace the Internet, however, has been undermined by growing anxiety about privacy and data collection. The 2013–14 revelations by Edward Snowden, the former CIA analyst who exposed wholesale government scrutiny of Internet communications, has deterred some users from going online at all, while discouraging web-enthusiasts from communicating any sort of information that they fear might be compromised.

Lane Fox raised her concerns about the chilling effect of data collection in a 2014 speech to the House of Lords, where she sits as a cross-bench peer. Debating the government's Data Retention and Investigatory Powers bill, she warned that freedoms promised by the web were in danger of being eroded. Urging Parliament to consider the implications of data collection, the role of surveillance and the trade-off between privacy and security, she expressed alarm at policy provisions that 'would allow for the blanket interception of all data from international technology companies meaning, in effect, that all of an individual's activity online is accessible to government'.

Governments around the world, notably in Brazil and Germany, reacted with alarm when it emerged that the US intelligence agencies were listening in to telephone traffic of foreign leaders, and gathering vast amounts of data from online social networks. Controversy over such data collection intensified in November 2014, when Robert Hannigan, the new head of GCHQ, the UK government's electronic surveillance agency, called on Internet users to reconsider the use of social networks or technology platforms that were also 'command and control' outlets for terrorist organisations.

Lane Fox regards this as a 'lazy argument', trying to equate the vast array of online discourse with potential threats to national security. She wants tighter regulations around what governments can collect, and how privacy should be protected.

'You should start from the premise that this is my data, and I choose to give it to governments, not the other way round,' she argues. 'If they want to spy on me, they need a warrant and to use the normal channels. I would feel as violated knowing that someone had been rootling around in my hard drive as I would if they had been rootling around in my desk at home. Yet we have this weird sense of a private space in our home, but no privacy when it comes to your private space online.'

Her words carry weight, as Lane Fox was previously the UK government's Digital Champion, working with the Cabinet Office to improve the delivery of public services using the web. She also served on an independent panel set up by Nick Clegg, the deputy prime minister, to propose a new framework for oversight of the UK security services.

Her vision for how the Internet should operate is reflected in five key principles drafted by the Web We Want campaign. Those principles aim to ensure freedom of expression online and offline; to guarantee affordable access to universally available communications platforms; to ensure the protection of personal user information and the right to communicate in private; to provide a decentralised and open infrastructure; and, finally, to provide networks that do not discriminate against content and users.

Those campaigning for such principles see three major hurdles to that vision: governments are not doing enough to provide full access and provide digital skills; fears over data collection are deterring online information-sharing; and the grip of huge – mainly US platforms – is dampening a risk-taking entrepreneurial culture.

Lane Fox admits that this last point is paradoxical. There are few companies as free-wheeling and entrepreneurial as Google or Facebook. But their success and enormous financial firepower act as a brake on Internet diversity, not least by acquiring a wide array of start-ups or rival technology platforms that might, in future, pose a competitive threat:

'Google backs talent and they buy businesses that they think will be successful, which is a way of hiring the best people to be on their side. It would be a rare British investor or entrepreneur that would turn down an astonishingly big US offer.'

Lane Fox and Brent Hoberman, the co-founders of lastminute.com, followed that path in 2005 when they sold the online travel and leisure platform to US technology and travel group Sabre. She insists that her exit was not simply cashing in; it coincided with her own near-death experience. In 2004, Lane Fox was badly injured in a car accident in Morocco, leaving her with a shattered pelvis and twenty-eight broken bones.

'I don't regret selling lastminute at all,' she says. 'My own personal situation was so peculiar because I was in hospital and so nearly dead. But I'm proud that it still exists. I'd be gutted if the brand had died.'

She hopes that the sort of risk-taking that spawned lastminute, and her latest start-up ventures, will be reinvigorated by the availability of more venture capitalism in Europe to match the investment culture of Silicon Valley. Financial institutions such as Santander and technology groups including Google are vowing to invest more in European start-ups. Alternative funding is also emerging from crowd-sharing platforms such as Kickstarter and Crowdcube.

If European countries are to incubate Internet platforms that prove a real alternative to the social power of Facebook or the retail dominance of Amazon or China's Alibaba, they may need to explore applications in new areas such as healthcare or education – services outside the mainstream of social networks.

'This is where there is an opportunity,' says Lane Fox. 'Unless we fundamentally restructure or redesign these public services, there is no way we are going to be able to save money. And it will be totally unfeasible to do that without starting with the web.'

Given those challenges and the systemic problem of slowing Internet penetration, she predicts a period of online disruption and confusion as new models and services undergo experimentation. To successfully navigate the next generation of the Internet will require closer collaboration between governments and private enterprise and users, especially regarding privacy, as well as co-operation among network operators and infrastructure companies to deliver universal access.

Lane Fox is cautiously optimistic that access and digital literacy will improve. If those factors fall into place, she says the outlook will be brighter in 2020:

'If we achieve what's needed in the UK, we will have a much more highly skilled workforce that is much more technically literate. We will have one of the best infrastructures in the world, radically different service delivery by government, more interaction with citizens and more political engagement. And we should have lots more start-ups that could become big European and global success stories. That's the prescription; easy. All we have to do is deliver those things; that's the hard part.'

Second opinion: the analysts' view

Early in 2015, Michel Combes, chief executive of telecommunications group Alcatel-Lucent, surprised his audience at a technology seminar in Israel by forecasting the arrival of 'digital skin'.

'In the next five to ten years I predict the end of smartphones. We will all have wearables and look at texts and videos on screens on our body, which will be like a kind of digital skin that will be connected on a permanent basis to the network.' According to Combes, 'Those networks will be faster and faster. It means that digital transmission will be like air, available everywhere, with billions of objects connected. And the network will be much closer to you, like fibre to your pocket.'

The ongoing technology revolution, which shows no sign of slowing down, is creating huge value for the companies building the devices, software and systems serving the industry. Towards the end of 2014, Apple hit a new record for market capitalisation – surpassing $700 billion – almost twice the size of Google, itself worth more than all the leading traditional US media companies combined. In the fourth quarter of 2014, Apple reaffirmed its pre-eminence in the technology industry by reporting record profits of $18 billion after selling 74 million smartphones in the last three months of the year.

Part of Apple's success has been its ability to refresh its products regularly, delivering incremental device improvements that at least match or exceed the innovation of rivals. The inability to fund such innovation has been the undoing of rivals such as Blackberry, whilst other companies such as Sony or IBM have retreated from some products (laptops) rather than compete with Apple as consumers migrate to newer devices.

Companies such as Apple in devices or Facebook in social media can justify their valuations by pointing to huge customer numbers and rising revenues. For many other technology companies, market capitalisations are a bet on the future.

The calculated gamble is that valuations will rise in line with demand for more intuitive and personalised technologies, and growing Internet penetration in emerging markets. The market research firm eMarketer predicts that more than 42 per cent of the world's population – 2.9 billion people – will be online in 2015, rising to an estimated 3.6 billion in 2018.

But access does not equate necessarily to literacy. Even in supposedly connected markets such as the UK and the US, the ability of large sections of the population to make use of apps and harness the Internet fully remains limited. In other large markets such as China, with an estimated 750 million users likely to be online by the end of the decade, censorship and restricted access are major issues.

This means that the future of technology will depend increasingly on twin levers of activity: better digital education of users and better traffic management. Kevin McElearney, senior vice president of Network Engineering for Comcast, the US cable group, told Alcatel-Lucent's 2014 Technology Symposium, that rising demand for video content was putting a strain on existing 'pipes' that handle digital communications:

'We have to double capacity every twenty-four months and we can't do that by just throwing capital at it. It's about how do you deliver smart traffic.'

But improved traffic management and faster connection speeds are just one part of the technology challenge. More importantly, perhaps, confidence must be restored among consumers following revelations of government spying, and malicious hacking by, allegedly, regimes such as North Korea. Trust in digital communication has declined just as usage has increased.

Restoring such trust will not be easy, not least because a small coterie of US technology companies appears to be profiting disproportionately from the world's desire to be connected, compared with the rest of the IT software, hardware and social media sector. Clearly, more cash will be generated by the top companies. In theory more value will be created by digitisation if the benefits of new technologies begin to penetrate areas such as public services and heavy industry. But that may require government intervention in an industry where the role of the state is regarded with suspicion by many users. The net result may be that the benefits of technology – both in wealth creation and IT access – will be far from universal for some time to come.

Jacob Wallenberg, Investor AB

Net asset value: $31.5 billion
Operating profit margin: 20%
Number of employees: 14,600
Number of markets served: N/A
Headquarters: Stockholm

The chairman of Investor AB will mark his tenth year in the role in 2015. He took on the chairmanship after leading positions at other companies in the Investor sphere. These included periods as chief executive and later chairman of Skandinaviska Enskilda Banken (SEB), the Swedish bank, and as vice-chairman of engineering group Atlas Copco. Wallenberg is a former non-executive director of the Coca-Cola Company. He remains vice-chairman of both SAS, the Scandinavian airline, and Ericsson, the telecommunications group. The graduate of the Wharton School at the University of Pennsylvania is also a board member of engineering group ABB, the Knut and Alice Wallenberg Foundation – which distributes funds for medical and educational research, and the Stockholm School of Economics.

Jacob Wallenberg has an over-riding vision for northern Europe's largest industrial holding group. It is the art of managing the 'two Cs': continuity and change. The chairman of Investor AB is a multi-tasking business leader. Together with his brother Peter Jr and his cousin Marcus, he plays the multiple roles of long-term and engaged shareholder, plural board member, benefactor for scientific research and guardian of a century-old family dynasty; his father, the family patriarch Peter Wallenberg, died in early 2015.

In those multiple roles, he chairs a Swedish investment company with significant stakes in businesses such as Atlas Copco; ABB, the Swiss–Swedish engineering giant; pharmaceutical group AstraZeneca; Electrolux; Saab; and Scandinavian bank SEB. He is also vice-chairman at Ericsson, the telecommunications group, in which Investor has a shareholding worth more than SKr13 billion ($1.7 billion). He plays the same role on the board of Scandinavian Airlines (SAS) and is a non-executive director of ABB. If that were not enough, he is also a director of the Knut and Alice Wallenberg Foundation, which is Europe's second-largest distributor of research funding after the Wellcome Trust.

Investor has a boardroom presence in and shareholder influence over companies with a combined market capitalisation of more than $200 billion. It exercises that influence, in many cases, through split shareholder structures whereby it owns greater voting rights than ordinary share capital. Although such structures are frowned upon in some markets, they enable Investor to remain a long-term force for continuity in Sweden, where it has shareholdings in companies accounting for about 40 per cent of the total stock market.

Many of those companies, such as Ericsson, Electrolux and ABB, have become global exporters and manufacturers. They are a testament to Sweden's economic history of developing strong engineering companies that were, from their inception, forced to look to international markets for growth given the small size of the domestic sector.

'We are engaged owners with a long-term view,' he says. 'But long term really does not mean that we are not impatient in the short term. We are dynamic owners.

'To deliver long-term stability – which is our ultimate goal – every day you have to look at your cash generation, your working capital, your balance sheet structure, your management talent, your R&D spending, your marketing. All these pieces have to be in place or you're not going to be successful in a global, competitive and challenging environment.'

He also defends the split shareholder structure that enables Investor to exercise a degree of control over the 'continuity and change' agenda at companies in the Wallenberg sphere: 'There are different ownership models in the world. A and B shares are one model – which also exist in other parts of the world such as the US – where the original owner, investor or entrepreneur has taken a risk and wants to retain an influence on the company. Not all of our underlying companies have A and B shares, including ABB and AstraZeneca. But I believe that A and B shares have allowed for the long-term success of Swedish industry.'

Wallenberg is the latest family member, with his cousin and brother, to manage this industrial matrix. It dates back to 1856 when A. O. Wallenberg, his great-great grandfather, founded Stockholm's Enskilda Bank (SEB). In the Swedish recession of 1877, the bank acquired parts of its industrial portfolio by swapping debt-for-equity in distressed companies. Almost forty years later, Investor AB was founded after the Swedish government forced the bank to demerge its corporate holdings. Some of those holdings were later transferred to the Knut and Alice Wallenberg Foundation, which was formed in 1917 and which remains the single largest shareholder in Investor.

Since then, SEB, Investor and the Wallenberg family foundations have emerged as some of the most enduring asset managers in European business and finance. In overseeing what Swedish commentators call 'the family sphere', today's Investor chairman shares power with his cousin Marcus, who is chairman of SEB and Saab, as well as Jacob's younger brother, Peter, who chairs Foundation Asset Management (FAM). FAM is the privately held family company that distributes dividends from its holdings to scientific research and education. Like his elder sibling, Peter sits on several boards. And like Investor, FAM also holds influential stakes in several companies, including paper group Stora Enso and engineering company SKF.

This division of responsibilities reflects a family tradition dating back generations. If one branch of the family was overseeing the bank, the other would manage the industrial assets. Collectively, they pursued the returns that would both reward shareholders and sustain the foundations established to support scientific research.

'Today there are three family members in different parts of the business and all of us are on the board of Investor,' says Wallenberg. 'We have continuous internal discussions about the directions to take. It works pretty seamlessly.'

Family businesses tend to be prone to disagreements over succession and inheritance planning. The Wallenbergs are no exception, although past power struggles have occasionally led to unintended consequences. In 1917, a childless K. A. Wallenberg created the foundations that have long underpinned Swedish scientific research, rather than distribute his wealth to other members of the family. Among them, Raoul Wallenberg opted for a diplomatic career in the 1930s, in which he famously used his position at the Swedish embassy in Hungary to help save thousands of Jews from the Holocaust before disappearing into Soviet custody after the war.

Today there are no such family divisions or controversies. Jacob says the 'family triumvirate' shares a common vision for both Investor and FAM: 'Our objective is to build the net asset value of the portfolio, to operate efficiently and pay a steadily rising dividend. If we get that right, it drives attractive total returns for our shareholders, hence the foundations at Investor are able to make research grants.'

The foundations have almost SKr70 billion ($8.5 billion) of assets under management, and in 2014 they will pay close to SKr2 billion ($242 million), compared with SKr1.76 billion ($213 million) in the previous year. Recipients include scientists conducting molecular and clinical research as well as basic research at university level, life sciences and advanced mathematics.

The net asset value of Investor's holdings surpassed SKr260 billion

($31.5 billion) in 2014. The income they generated has delivered annualised total shareholder returns of 14 per cent since the mid-1990s. Those returns have been driven primarily by investment and asset holdings in four broad business clusters: IT and telecommunications, industrial engineering, financial services and pharmaceuticals. More recently, Investor acquired wholly-owned unlisted companies, particularly in healthcare, an area where it expanded through the acquisition of Aleris, a wholly-owned operator of care homes and medical facilities across Scandinavia.

Wallenberg says the holding company is now contemplating two broad new areas of activity: consumer-orientated manufacturing and social care. Explaining the potential switch to consumer goods, he points out: 'If you look at Electrolux, it was always a nuts and bolts company in the past. It was a matter of production planning and efficient production lines. Now it is about design, convenience and software, everything that makes a product more interesting to the individual consumer.'

Electrolux's presence in consumer goods has grown with the proposed acquisition (at time of going to press) of GE's appliances businesses, significantly expanding its presence in the US. Wallenberg says this consumer focus also applies to holdings in Husqvarna, the world's largest producer of outdoor power products, and even SEB, the retail bank. In social care, meanwhile, Investor has diversified into education by investing in Kunskapsskolan – Sweden's largest operator of independent schools, with about 11,000 students in thirty-six schools.

Such investments have prompted criticism from left-of-centre parties and activists, who have argued that it should be the role of the welfare state, not private enterprise, to provide these services. That criticism intensified in Sweden's 2014 election campaign, which led to the removal of the centre-right coalition – replaced by one led by the centre-left Social Democrats, which had dominated Swedish politics for most of the twentieth century.

To Investor's dismay, the new government threatened to roll back privatisation in education and healthcare, and to impose regulations curbing their for-profit approach to such services. In response, the company used an interim management statement in 2014 to remind the government of basic business principles:

'Any company that wants to invest to develop its business needs to make a profit. Loss-making companies simply do not survive,' it said. 'The uncertainty induced by the government will likely hold back private investments in the sector and could even force some actors out – a bit paradoxically, as Sweden needs increased investment to meet the sharply rising demand from an ageing population and the need for improved availability.'

The intervention reflects the soft power wielded by the Wallenbergs in Sweden, where members of the family have previously served as government ministers and applied pressure on policies ranging from suffrage to international trade and nationalisation. The latest generation of family leaders are relatively apolitical in comparison to their forefathers. But they are ready to make their views known when party politics threaten to destabilise the country's business community.

Whether on welfare privatisation or addressing widespread public concern about immigration, Jacob Wallenberg calls for more clarity and action to address the long-term structural challenges created by an ageing population, worsening education results and cross-border migration.

Without making direct demands, he says: 'Sweden has to be a well-functioning society. We have a self-interest that the country where we are headquartered operates effectively and modernises in many different respects. This ultimately affects the background against which all these multinational companies, based in Sweden, take decisions be it education, R&D, deregulation and so forth.'

Wallenberg insists that Investor's formula for delivering growth and total shareholder returns will not be derailed by a minority left-of-centre government in the family's home country. He reiterates that the listed holding company and the family foundations will strive to build best-in-class companies, with stable long-term ownership and a commitment to R&D and innovation. He has little doubt that the 'family sphere' will continue to deliver on that vision.

That vision includes best-in-class corporate governance and encouraging the sort of gender diversity for which Scandinavia is famous. At Investor companies, however, there are few women chief executives, with the notable exception of Annika Falkengren at the SEB bank. Wallenberg says: 'I am against quotas for boards or senior management positions. It is very important to continue to attract women to senior positions and ultimately to boards. But quotas are not the solution to promote women to senior managerial positions. Every company has to develop a culture that allows women to have the same chances as men to be promoted. Companies have to have diversity on their top agenda.'

On such issues, Wallenberg radiates a quiet self-assurance and authority. The only chinks in his confidence in the Wallenberg formula relate to factors beyond the family's control. Whilst he is sure that Investor and the foundations can adapt to challenges posed by government policies, technology and the economic cycle, he is more pessimistic about the impact of geo-political tensions around the world. The Investor chairman, who is also a member of the Bildeberg forum of transatlantic business leaders, says, 'When it comes to geo-politics, I don't know where to start. I think the whole issue of the Middle East, the issues created by the rise of Islamic State and militant Islam, and anti-Western sentiment is of such magnitude that I don't see a solution.

'When you add in the changing equation of energy security, particularly as the United States becomes less dependent on imported oil and gas following its shale gas revolution, it could have a dramatic impact on the political and economic climate. It has implications for the Middle East, for American policy towards Israel, and for new constellations of political influence. Like so many others, I am scratching my head about where this is taking us. It's certainly into the unknown. Am I concerned? I am extremely concerned.'

That concern extends also to European integration and the functioning of the European Union. As one of the leading industrialists, arguably, in Scandinavia, Wallenberg argues for more co-ordination and leadership from the major EU economies such as Britain, France and Germany.

'Europe has to consolidate a lot more, with stronger leadership at the heart of the Union while observing the principle of subsidiarity. Britain has to continue to play a full role within the EU. It would do enormous damage to Europe if Britain would elect to leave. To have the axis of London, Berlin and Paris engaged in developing the union is key for European development. If that was left to an axis of Berlin and Paris, it would be a very different picture to the detriment of Europe as a whole.'

That uncertainty is compounded by concerns that China will no longer be a growth engine for European companies. Wallenberg, who is a member of an international advisory council to the mayor of Shanghai, says: 'The Chinese are becoming so competitive when it comes to costs, intellectual property rights and design that European business must take note.'

He predicts that European companies will need to strengthen their presence in the US, explore ties with emerging economies and reinforce their export and manufacturing presence in countries such as Turkey, Mexico and Indonesia.

'Whatever the geo-political climate and regulatory environment, at the end of the day it comes down to delivering growth,' he argues. 'In order to generate the basis for growth, your products have to be market-able and advanced, which makes R&D absolutely fundamental if you are going to succeed in penetrating these semi-new markets. Alongside all of this, I need a strong balance sheet with not too much tied up in net working capital. If I did that, there would be a risk of having some short-term activist chasing me down the road. So as an owner it is imperative to always be on the ball. We need to continuously adapt to market conditions to deliver value to our shareholders.'

The primary spur behind all this effort is not private wealth creation, according to long-term followers of the Wallenberg family. In his book *The Family that Shaped Sweden's Economy*, the author and academic Gunnar Wetterberg writes:

'Members of the present generation have substantial incomes and considerable wealth but in neither respect are they among the foremost in Sweden. Their leading position derives instead from economic power, gathered in institutions and companies, wielded in boardrooms and manifested in opportunities and room for manoeuvre, rather than simply in billions of krona and thousands of employees.'

Jacob Wallenberg declines to comment on how the family exercises its power or its personal wealth. He regards his management role – and that of his brother Peter and cousin Marcus – as much more about asset management, delivering returns to Investor's 150,000 non-family shareholders, and generating dividend income for distribution to the scientific community.

'These are the key things that I think about every morning,' he says. 'Today we have a fairly well-consolidated position. Our balance sheets are in order, the businesses are doing well, and they are generating good cash and dividend pools. My hope is that there are individuals in the next generation who will qualify to be part of that job managing those assets. Do I see a dramatic shift of direction, or are we going to invest in different pools of assets, or are we going to change our risk profile? It's a very simple answer: no.'

Instead, the Investor chairman intends to remain focused on the vision of creating long-term sustainable returns from the listed and unlisted assets in the portfolio. He reiterates that achieving those returns will depend on a zealous commitment to financial and operational efficiency as well as R&D efficiency, and a willingness to seize opportunities for accretive deals.

In pursuit of that vision, he points out that the Wallenbergs have never held on to assets for sentimental or emotional reasons but only in the best interest of the individual company. Rather, they have been willing deal-makers when necessary: merging Asea and Brown Boveri to create ABB, combining Astra with Zeneca, and Stora with Enso in the paper industry. The family sold control of Saab Automobile to General Motors before its eventual demise; disposed of Investor's stake in Scania in VW; and acquired unlisted assets in the healthcare and medical sectors, among several others, while expanding into new areas such as education.

Wallenberg doubts the company will face the sort of revolutionary changes that the family encountered generations ago, despite his anxieties about geo-political uncertainty, the potential anti-business policies of the Swedish government and schisms in the European Union. Against that backdrop, he sees his role as one of sophisticated maintenance – keeping the family business working efficiently for the next generation.

'When it comes to dramatic shifts, I am not sure we will see anything of the magnitude that our grandfather faced,' he predicts. 'Our grandfather and his brother lived through two world wars. They witnessed the industrial revolution, evolution of the combustion engine, the computer, the arrival of aviation.

'We may not face those sorts of change. Clearly, there will be major opportunities and significant challenges such as digitalisation and automation that might completely change production. Am I concerned? Of course I'm concerned. But that is part of management and leadership, isn't it? You must be able to deal with the unknown.'

Second opinion: the analysts' view

Shareholder activism has become a toxic moniker in parts of society. The Hollywood version, frequently re-circulated by the tabloid press, portrays sharp-suited corporate raiders buying and selling companies, stripping assets and jeopardising jobs in a remorseless search for capital.

The truth is far removed from that fiction. Today's corporate raiders are as likely to be physicists or mathematicians specialising in digital algorithms as they are instinctive investors hoping for alchemy. Investment holding companies, in contrast, tend to have a long ownership horizon – certainly longer than the nano-seconds governing the so-called 'algo' trades conducted by automated computer systems.

The common criticism of investment groups, including the Wallenberg vehicle Investor AB, is that they trade at a perennial discount to net asset value (NAV). Why invest in an investing company when its stock trades below the sum of the parts implied by the shareholdings it owns?

In reality, what you are paying for are the business smarts of the portfolio managers: the individuals who stitch together asset classes that ordinary investors would rarely pick. And also for the active management of stocks that they hold, often exercised by their ability to change management or redirect strategies through the exercise of their shares.

But unlike most shareholder activists, which tend to be concentrated in the US, Investor is a unique vehicle. Its collection of listed holdings has been built up over generations, and not because of short-term trading positions. Those positions out-live different generations of Wallenbergs, who prize continuity over the sort of quarterly returns promised by the likes of Berkshire Hathaway.

This sense of history and continuity was on show in February 2015, when the Swedish royal family and the country's political leadership turned out in force for the funeral of family patriarch Peter Wallenberg, father to Jacob and Peter Jr, and uncle to Marcus – the current generation of family leadership.

For the family and for Investor, the strategic goal of their core investments – the large listed companies that it influences and its wholly-owned operating assets – is to generate a return exceeding the market cost of capital. In the five years up to 2015, Investor shares have returned more than 22 per cent a year, and the discount to NAV has narrowed from a historic trough of 40 per cent in 2004 to less than 17 per cent.

Any shareholder would, therefore, have enjoyed a strong ride by hitching their wagon to Wallenberg strategic control. Given that the family is not expected to push for a major transformation of the portfolio comprising stakes in ABB, AstraZeneca and Electrolux, the investment case for the period to 2020 depends on growth assumptions at such holdings. AstraZeneca could be acquired, as Pfizer tried and failed to do in 2014, which would entail a healthy takeover premium. An expanded Electrolux could deliver some upside, as might Ericsson by upgrading its mobile phone infrastructure. But other assets, such as Atlas Copco and Wärtsilä, may struggle to grow and the discount may widen. According to one sell-side analyst, 'We see the current discount level as unsustainable, and believe it will expand back closer to its average levels.'

If the discount does widen again, it may raise questions over the logic of the assets held by Investor. But the family is unlikely to change its long-term positions even if it does so.

Generations of Wallenbergs have seen the NAV discount widen and narrow several times before. Over the last twenty years, the Investor B shares have delivered annual average returns of 13.5 per cent, rising to more than 20 per cent following recent market rallies. Bears could argue that such investment companies are merely trackers of overall market health. In contrast, bulls could claim that they are a positive influence on strong performance for each asset they own. The truth lies, as always, between the two. But it would take a brave investor to bet against a family that has outlived numerous boom and bust cycles to deliver above-average returns.

Eduardo Leite, Baker & McKenzie

Annual revenues: $2.54 billion
Operating profit margin: 35.8%
Number of employees (including partners): 10,896
Number of markets served: 77 offices in 47 countries
Headquarters: Chicago, IL

The executive committee chairman at the world's largest law firm began practising in Brazil, where he remains a leading member of the country's bar association. He joined Baker & McKenzie in 1979 after graduating from the University of New York and the University of São Paulo and, prior to that, the University of Uruguay. In Brazil, he worked on almost all of the country's privatisations, particularly in the power and energy sector. Leite, fluent in five languages, led the law firm's global energy, mining and infrastructure industry group and the Latin American Regional Council. He has been a partner at Baker & McKenzie since 1986, is a member of the international business leaders' advisory council for the mayor of Beijing, and in 2014, he was re-elected chairman by his fellow partners.

When it comes to the rule of law, Sudan has a poor record. A functioning legal system was one of many institutions that barely survived the Sudanese civil war, which cost millions of lives and displaced many more before the 2005 ceasefire.

Peace treaties are not part of the normal client service at Baker & McKenzie, the world's largest law firm. Yet Baker & McKenzie lawyers were among those who analysed and helped draft a suitable framework agreement, paving the way for a comprehensive peace treaty between the government in Khartoum and the Sudan People's Liberation Movement. The firm's *International Negotiations Handbook*, a seventy-page blueprint for peace talks, has since become required reading for conflict mediators.

Legal experts call Baker & McKenzie the 'United Nations of law firms'. There are no plans for a Sudanese practice – US sanctions would prohibit it – but the firm now operates in several cities where international lawyers were once a rarity, including Yangon, Almaty, Baku and Ho Chi Minh City. These city practices contribute to a network of seventy-seven offices in more than forty-five countries.

'We want to be a firm without nationality, if such a thing is possible,' says Eduardo Leite, the Brazilian lawyer who chairs Baker & McKenzie's executive committee. 'Laws are very local, whether you are in Myanmar or Mexico. But the practice of law is global, and so are we.'

When the firm held its 2014 annual meeting in London, it took three hotels to accommodate the 1,430 partners. Collectively, they generate more than $2.5 billion in annual revenues. Profits per equity partner reached almost $1.3 million in the fiscal year ending 30 June 2014, according to the journal *American Law Daily*. Both revenues and profits are today a far cry from the small partnership founded by Chicago lawyer Russell Baker in 1949.

Baker built his legal career advising US companies on tax policies. But he believed there was a gap in the market to serve corporate clients in multiple jurisdictions. In the 1940s, he persuaded John McKenzie, a Chicago trial lawyer, to give up his work as in-house counsel defending taxi companies to form a new firm advising US industrial groups. While

Baker set about opening offices overseas, McKenzie continued litigating cases in Chicago that funded the international expansion. In its first year, Baker & McKenzie earned $89,000 in fees, of which $51,000 was divided among the lawyers in net profits.

By the time of McKenzie's death in 1962, the firm was operating in ten offices from Caracas to Amsterdam, and London to Mexico City. Fifteen years later, when Baker passed away, the network was approaching thirty offices. The total reached forty by 1988 and sixty at the millennium.

When the partners gathered for their 2014 meeting in London, they celebrated the opening of new offices in Brisbane, Dubai, Yangon and Jeddah. They also voted to reappoint Leite as chairman for another term – a period in which he has vowed to build what he calls a 'three-dimensional global matrix'. His vision is to cement Baker & McKenzie's position among the global elite of the legal industry. That will involve more cross-border client teams, a greater focus on cyber security, deeper relationship management, the recruitment of outside experts to strengthen different practice areas and a disciplined approach to costs.

All this, he says, is symptomatic of the changing nature of the law and client relationships. An industry in which the top 100 firms generate annual revenues of more than $88 billion has seen a dramatic change in the way it operates.

'We are not agnostic like the old days,' explains Leite. 'Back then, the relationship was for the lawyer to say: "Tell me the facts and I'll tell you the law – or if it's a grey area we'll file for a ruling." Today, everyone is trying to build long-term institutional relationships.'

Baker & McKenzie is discreet about those relationships. You will find no client list on the wall of the firm's Chicago headquarters. At the fiftieth floor reception at 300 East Randolph Street, visitors talk in hushed tones, perhaps infected by the air of confidentiality. The only rapid movement comes from the black water feature, which stretches across the floor. Leite jokes that the firm had to install a ripple mechanism in the pool because some visitors mistook the surface for polished marble: 'We were giving advice and paying for client shoes.'

From his Chicago office, Leite explains the key components of his

three-dimensional global matrix. At its heart is a global key client programme focused on the firm's top fifty clients: 'We have to nurture
relationships in the greatest number of jurisdictions that produce not just
large fees but complex deals and complex cross-border litigation. In the
past five years, we have seen some firms dissolve or go bankrupt because
they relied on clients that were neither long term nor institutional.'

Baker & McKenzie has avoided that pitfall by producing, training,
recruiting and retaining lawyers with three-dimensional careers.

'The first dimension is to be an expert or to focus on one area of
law, such as corporate, international trade or tax, for example,' says the
chairman. 'Second is to have a certain inclination and willingness to learn
about a specific industry, such as pharmaceuticals or finance. And third
is the client – we want lawyers to focus on a few clients and to learn
all about them.'

As part of its matrix strategy, Baker & McKenzie envisions focusing
on industrial sectors that it expects to generate legal demand. There are
four broad sectors that are expected to drive activity at the firm in the
period to 2020: energy, mining and infrastructure; IT and communications; pharmaceuticals and healthcare; and financial.

There are other industrial practice areas that earn lucrative fees,
including automotive, retail, entertainment and luxury goods. But Leite
says, 'We see these four as long-term, fast-growth and requiring high-end
legal advice. It has been an attempt to move from commodity work like
reviewing thousands and thousands of contracts to, instead, litigating to
help a client transform their business in one way or another.'

Areas in which the firm aims to deliver value to such clients include
international arbitration, sanctions, compliance, mergers and acquisitions
and cyber security. This last area has become critical, particularly for the
information technology industry, where privacy rules and data collection
laws are not aligned between the US and Europe and remain completely
different in Southeast Asia.

Baker & McKenzie is even helping governments in some emerging
markets to draft privacy laws, particularly where there is little case law
or precedent.

'Lawyers can influence the enactment and the drafting of laws,' says Leite. 'And they do it with industry knowledge and aligned with clients, because they are the ones who tell us what the issue is or provide the information we need.'

Below the top fifty clients, the firm has identified a second tier of another 150 key clients that it services with virtual teams in multiple countries. Typically, a global client will be served by three senior partners, one based in North America, one in Asia and one in Europe, backed up by a team of up to sixty lawyers from all over the world, each of whom must have a business plan to deal with the client and understand their strategy.

Competition for those clients and to retain them over the long term has intensified significantly since the financial crisis of 2008. When the crisis hit, business started to dry up in areas such as transactions, litigation and cross-border ventures. Given the reputational challenge to many companies caught up in the crisis, particularly in financial services, the importance of the legal department and the general counsel function also rose dramatically. But the increase in legal anxiety at the height of the financial crisis did not lead to a fee bonanza. In an era of austerity and cost-cutting, clients began reviewing fees as cash-strapped procurement officers demanded savings.

In this perfect storm, many law firms collapsed or fell prey to takeover. Others joined forces in a period of merger mania as firms that were focused on one market or specialism sought critical mass and protective scale. Baker & McKenzie was among those firms of a size, international spread and range of services to survive the industry shake-out, along with rivals such as DLA Piper, Kirkland & Ellis, and Skadden, Arps, Slate, Meagher & Flom. But Leite believes the market adjustment is not over. There will be further consolidation.

'We are going the way of other industries in professional services like accounting. I don't think we'll end up with the "big four" like that, but there is going to be a global elite of ten large global firms.'

The financial crisis and the ensuing impact on the legal industry, with attendant pressure on business demand and fees, exposed two structural issues that could disrupt the vision that Leite and other firm leaders have for the future. One concerns the mobility of people, and where legal expertise is concentrated.

According to a study of international asset classes by McKinsey, talented people proved one of the least mobile segments, especially compared with technology, trade and financial assets experts. There is a trade imbalance in lawyers: an over-supply of top legal talent in North America and Europe when most of the demand is coming from Southeast Asia, China, Africa and South America.

'There's a real difficulty, a challenge, to get the right talent to move good European lawyers to Africa; Australians to Asia or good American lawyers to go from north to south,' according to the Baker & McKenzie chairman.

The second big challenge is about developing the next generation of legal talent in a climate where clients are less willing to pay billable hours for newly-qualified lawyers to learn on the job. This has created a vicious circle whereby firms are reducing the number of junior attorneys they hire each year because the cost of training them is not recoverable in the way it used to be. This means that law schools are still producing a high number of graduates who are not so employable.

Leite predicts that a new model will be required, requiring a degree of consensus between clients' in-house legal departments, law schools and firms such as Baker & McKenzie, and government – which has significant demand for well-trained attorneys. His vision of the solution involves law schools producing graduates better prepared to be productive from day one, rather than requiring practical training from their first employer. Law firms, in turn, will need to reduce the weight given to whether a junior attorney is covering their costs with hours billed and collected.

'In-house legal departments will need to deal with the misconception that new graduates do not add value, and they need to do more training of their own,' says Leite. 'The same, more or less, goes for the government.'

In the meantime, and in the absence of such reform, firms such as

Baker & McKenzie are looking at how to harness technology to address the lack of senior-level mobility. And they are looking at ways to lower the cost of service with better modelling and more focused relationship management.

'We are using technology like client relationship management tools and new technologies to measure what's happening with our clients: how we work together, identifying potential projects and where they are taking place,' he adds. 'I think the next step is to emulate the auto parts manufacturers, and look at how they maximised efficiency in a highly competitive industry where margins were crunched, by becoming indispensable to the end producers.'

It is not exactly clear how efficiencies will be achieved. Baker & McKenzie hopes to overcome the challenges facing the legal industry by giving more power to its global director of pricing. Leite's task is to maximise the return on the firm's ultimate unit of value: billable hours. As part of the efficiency drive, the firm is also bringing in outside experts – sometimes non-lawyers – to bolster the quality of its client teams in the core industry growth areas. Some are part-time advisors, project managers, industry specialists, academics or economists. 'They become part of the team, and they're profitable because they make sure they give client credibility on any given project.'

The firm is also investing in technologies and cyber experts, believing that cyber security will become one of the sector growth areas of the future. The cyber specialists recruited by the firm work across multiple practice areas, reflecting the shared anxiety in all businesses regarding data security, privacy breaches and infiltration: 'The risk for a client is massive class action and litigation. The investigations are huge and can cost a fortune. So clients must have policies and technical protection in place.

'That involves a lot of work on litigation, prevention, consumer privacy and data security. This issue is now of broad concern among clients, because once you have a breach – whether it's a consumer company, a retailer, a credit-card issue or even a government agency – the consequences are terrible.'

Baker & McKenzie has beefed up its own security against hacking and intrusion, including three layers of encryptions, systems and filters to protect data. 'We have to use the top tools that our clients use, because if we don't have those in place we won't get hired,' adds Leite.

In this legal marketplace, demand is growing fast for service expertise in areas such as technology and emerging markets. To exploit that demand, Baker & McKenzie envisions an even bigger focus on industry practice groups and client relationships. This strategy is likely to see further international expansion, depending on client demand and the opening up of countries, such as Myanmar, where there are questions about investment rules, old embargos and local laws. The firm is expected to look even more strategically at how it manages and preserves key client relationships and avoids conflicts, and how it identifies the next speciality area where it needs new talent.

The difference between success and failure, according to the chairman, will depend on a formula – his 3D matrix – of international spread, industry expertise and specialist legal knowledge: 'Leadership in our market is about having global expertise that connects the best of the emerging world with mature jurisdictions, both in law and practice, and techniques that are completely attuned with what clients want.

'We have to be innovative in providing services and partnerships with our clients in which we can lower our cost of production whilst maintaining the absolute quality of what we deliver. We must not lose sight [of the fact] that law is a profession, as well as a business. The practice of law is what the Romans called *munus publicum* – a service to society – and if we go too far looking for profits we cease to be something essential: a force for stability.'

Second opinion: the analysts' view

Customer intimacy may be the marketing industry's latest buzz-phrase, but it is increasingly being applied to the legal profession.

Large firms in the so-called magic circle are devoting more resources to serving their most lucrative global clients, hoping to become indispensable advisers who are retained throughout the economic cycle and not on a case-by-case basis. To be indispensable requires global and industrial expertise, which is why firms are opening offices in new growth markets such as Myanmar and hiring non-lawyers with particular insights into different businesses.

Whilst geographic spread and industrial specialisms might suit Baker & McKenzie, it is not necessarily a model that suits other law firms or their clients. The world's largest law firm has to go on seeking scale and new ways to generate fees because of its sheer size. It has so many 'mouths to feed' that it has to keep growing.

This is the same burden that faces bulge bracket investment banks. Like banking, however, the overheads and cost of using the largest firms creates opportunities for the rise of smaller more specialist boutiques, which can eat away at both fees and clients. To counter that threat, larger firms have to become more adept at managing both bureaucracy and costs.

'Law firms increasingly are outsourcing administrative, clerical and technical support jobs to third-party providers and overseas support centers where wages are often much lower,' according to M. P. McQueen of *The American Lawyer*. In addition to changes to cost structures, a growing number of law firms are expected to change their remuneration terms for senior client-handlers. This could lead to the replacement of the traditional partnership model – where rewards are shared equally – to a performance-related pay structure. This would require new ways to measure returns-per-partner, as billable hours may no longer accurately reflect an individual's contribution to a firm's success.

Changes to law firms' compensation structures, international reach and back-office operations all reflect efforts to secure fees in a volatile marketplace for advisory services. But firms are also exploring new practice areas to drive long-term profitability, which Patrick McKenna, a leading North American consultant on law firm practice, predicts could include 'cutting-edge areas such as drone law and personalised medicine'.

Expansion in such areas signals how legal services must adapt to the mega-trends affecting clients. As with other industries, these include the pressures created by mass urbanisation – especially in emerging markets – ageing populations, increasingly globalised trade and the need for enhanced transport links, communications, financial services and modern healthcare provision.

Legal columnist Aric Press says: 'To cope with these new realities, among other things the private sector and government will have to make major advances in the life sciences, create financial markets to aid a teetering population, and build infrastructure that will support the dense life of the world's cities. All of that is work that will require intense doses of legal help. For intellectual property, financial services and project finance practices, the best is yet to come.'

Maybe so, but maintaining world-class legal services in such areas will also depend on the ability of firms to nurture and retain top lawyers with the experience and qualifications to meet client expectations. This exposes the catch-22 of the industry: it is finding it harder to persuade clients to pay for junior attorneys' time – with a domino effect on in-house training. And firms are finding it harder to identify the rainmakers of the future when the supply of qualified but inexperienced lawyers far exceeds current client demand. It will require firms of genuine scale to address that problem, thus implying that smaller legal outfits may face a trying period ahead.

Beth Comstock, GE

....

Annual revenues: $148.6 billion
Operating profit margin: 11.2%
Number of employees: 305,000
Number of markets served: 170 countries
Headquarters: Fairfield, CT

....

When the chief marketing officer of GE was appointed in 2003, she was the first executive to hold the position in twenty years. She joined the leadership of the global industrial and financial group from NBC Universal, the former media subsidiary of GE. There, Comstock led the early development of Hulu, the TV industry's first online streaming service, in her role as head of ad-sales, marketing and research. Before NBC, she also worked at rival media companies CBS and Turner Broadcasting, now part of Time Warner. At GE, she now leads the group strategy in marketing, sales, licensing and communications. Comstock also oversees GE Ventures, the division that partners with start-up technology companies. She is a board member at Nike and Quirky, the online hub for new technology inventions.

In a hospital in rural China, not far from Chengdu, doctors and nurses are working alongside non-medical staff seconded from a distant corporation. Product designers, engineers and technology specialists from GE – that most capitalist of industrial groups – are supporting communist state health workers to review equipment standards and care quality.

The project, part of China's willing embrace of state-sponsored capitalism, is regarded as an important marketing coup by GE. The US industrial and financial giant envisions getting closer and closer to its customers over the coming years. Customer intimacy, a new watchword at GE, is being encouraged. A customer who regards the group as indispensable and responsive is a customer more likely to buy GE products.

'When you embed a team in a rural hospital in China, they are able to see things that even the best physician and nurse can't tell you because they're watching behaviours,' says Beth Comstock, chief marketing officer at GE. 'They see how patient monitors are being used in intensive care. And they are able to create new product offers, new solutions that the hospitals couldn't figure out how to solve.'

Under the marketing initiative in China, feedback from Sichuan province is relayed to product developers in GE's healthcare division, who use the information to upgrade services and equipment sold to hospitals around the world. It is an example of how GE is changing its marketing efforts and customer relationship management. In future, it wants customers to be involved in product development and innovation, raising their concerns at a much earlier stage of GE's research and development efforts.

The stakes are high at GE. In healthcare alone, the group boasts quarterly revenues of more than $4 billion and operating margins of 16 per cent. Marketing efforts to enhance healthcare sales are being mirrored in GE's six other industrial divisions, comprising power and water, oil and gas, energy management, aviation, transport and appliances and lighting. Together, those businesses generate total quarterly sales of more than $26 billion. A further $10 billion of quarterly revenues are generated from the GE Capital finance business, which is being demerged in 2015 into a separately-listed US entity called Synchrony Financial.

Comstock, who leads the group's global marketing, sales and

licensing operations as well as GE Ventures, says that growing customer intimacy – whether in rural China or industrial New Jersey – will be central to increasing GE's worldwide sales over the next five years.

'Business-to-business marketing has always been about delivering value and innovation; now it's about intimacy too. We have to be essential to our customers. GE cannot be more essential than to be the company that creates the aircraft engines that power your airline, or the locomotive that runs your railroad, the oil and gas drilling machinery that runs your oilfield or the power generation equipment that is vital for your utility business. So this demands a level of intimacy and insight that, frankly, I think we've overlooked for decades.'

When Comstock was appointed in 2003, she was GE's first chief marketing officer in more than twenty years. The former President of Integrated Media at NBC Universal, then a GE subsidiary, had the task of upgrading and simplifying GE's vast sales and marketing efforts. Her efforts formed part of a sweeping reorganisation strategy led by Jeff Immelt, the chief executive who took over GE's reins from his legendary predecessor, Jack Welch.

Immelt's streamlining saw GE withdraw from areas such as plastics and media. In 2014, it agreed to sell its household appliances business to Electrolux of Sweden. The demerger of the US financial services will reduce GE's complexity still further. Comstock says the spate of divestments – culminating in the 2015 IPO of Synchrony Financial – will transform GE into a much simpler global technology business in each of the industrial segments that it serves. But a leaner GE will not be an end in itself. It has to grow. So Comstock wants the company to become much better at explaining its business proposition.

'You can't sell if you can't tell,' she says simply. 'I think technology companies often want to lead with all the amazing things their technology can do, not the benefit of what it delivers. If you are just a complicated portfolio and you don't know what the outcome is, it's harder to tell the story. So now, at GE, we are moving to a model based on outcomes. We need to show the value that we deliver, as well as the financial outcome for investors and the positive outcome for customers.'

With Immelt's blessing, Comstock has set about transforming marketing from an overhead cost to an operating function that creates revenue opportunities. That has meant embedding marketing specialists not only with customers – as in Chengdu – but also in research and product development, engineering, testing and purchasing. As part of this new marketing vision, customer needs will be integrated at a much earlier stage of product development. In another sign of things to come, marketing executives are now dubbed 'explorers' – prospecting for the next product opportunity that will stimulate additional sales.

Although pockets of internal resistance to this new approach remain, Comstock maintains that a growing proportion of GE engineers are embracing the marketing mantra of getting relevant products to customers much faster.

'They are starting to ask themselves: how do we make sure we're innovating with our customers; not just showing up when we think the product is perfect. We've seen too many times when too many features are embedded in products which were either too complicated, too technical or weren't able to deliver the experience and value that customers are going to pay for. That's got to end.'

The leadership of GE is also cultivating what it regards as a positive creative tension between marketing and product development. The company's marketing department traditionally saw its role as addressing customer demands, providing products to solve their needs. The product development teams, in contrast, wanted to bring the most technically-advanced products to market whether there was proven demand or not. 'Getting that tension in place is really hard. Everything needs to align around the customer and talking to them about what they want from us,' says Comstock.

Marketing efforts built on the principle of customer intimacy are being rolled out across the company. She cites the experience of GE marketing teams working in pre-natal medical facilities in Indonesia, which led to the development of portable ultrasound machines that could be trekked into remote regions. Or the case of a railroad, where Comstock claims that the ability to run trains one mile-per-hour faster can lead to network savings of $200 million a year. But she admits that GE cannot impose its marketing will or simplification mantra on unwilling customers, regions or potential acquisition targets.

In 2014, it learned that lesson the hard way with its $16.9 billion offer for Alstom of France. GE was forced to revise its offer when the French government reacted with dismay to the acquisition of a national champion in power generation and grid management. Faced with a rival potential offer for Alstom by Siemens of Germany, GE reconfigured its deal as a $13.5 billion takeover of Alstom's gas and steam turbines business, whilst forging three joint ventures with the French company in renewable energy equipment, grid systems and nuclear power.

By 2020, GE hopes the revised deal with Alstom will generate synergy savings of $1.2 billion a year through combined sourcing, integrated R&D and consolidated support functions in areas such as marketing. Announcing the revised proposal, Immelt said: 'Our synergies remain intact. It is immediately accretive to our earnings, furthers the transition of our portfolio towards industrial businesses, and broadens our product and service offerings for customers.'

Behind the hyperbole, there was some hard bargaining. In return for sanctioning the new deal, the French government persuaded GE to sell its rail signalling business to the remaining independent Alstom business – which will focus wholly on railway trains and equipment. The French state also secured a preferred share and veto rights over a 50–50 alliance between GE and Alstom in global nuclear and steam turbine equipment.

Comstock describes the Alstom negotiations and ultimate deal outcome as an example of GE's ability 'to pivot'. This is not seen as an admission of defeat, rather a test of flexibility. If GE does not get its way with a strategy, it will pivot to secure its long-term ambitions by another route. The pivot culture is becoming embedded at GE following the company's embrace of a marketing programme called FastWorks. The programme, adapted from similar strategies in Silicon Valley, aims to integrate a start-up culture in GE decision making: 'One of the best Fastworks tools is this idea of the pivot. We start down one path and then end up going down another to get to our ultimate goal. It's the nature of progress that you must pivot.'

The pivot and customer intimacy are two of Comstock's strategic priorities in marketing GE around the world. The other three, which she expects to become hallmarks of GE over the next few years, are increasing development collaboration, more use of big data, and the industrialisation of the Internet. The chief marketing officer says increasing collaboration will be vital because GE admits it will not discover next-generation technologies or the next product breakthrough on its own.

'Whether you are a country, a government or a company, or an academic institution, the problems we are trying to address are just too big to go it alone. We must collaborate with more partners.'

GE also acknowledges that start-ups, rather than aged conglomerates, are more entrepreneurial and faster to act in seizing new opportunities. So it has forged partnerships with companies such as Kaggle in data connectivity, as well as GrabCAD, the cloud-based engineering platform, and the so-called 'invention factory', Quirky. In recent years, GE has brought to market several product ideas that were developed by Quirky inventors, whom Comstock has asked to experiment in areas of GE activity. She is calling for more 'lean start-up' ideas from GE's new collaborators. These collaborators include partly-owned or GE-funded start-up companies that are grouped within the GE Ventures division: 'It's basically prototyping – an idea born in the software side of the business world that we've adapted to the hardware side.'

To ensure such prototypes turn into commercial reality, GE knows it must hire and retain more creative talent – the sort of entrepreneurs more commonly found in Silicon Valley than an industrial group. GE knows the sort of entrepreneurs it wants, but Comstock says 'we're all kind of scared by them'. She recognises that it will take time for increased collaboration and the recruitment of entrepreneurs to deliver a bottom-line benefit. But those benefits, when they arrive, should be broader than just generating cash and shareholder returns.

'Business is in business to make money. But the firm belief of most people running business is that it has to be executed with purpose,' she adds. 'Innovation and profitability has to be tethered to a purpose. We're not just making it for the sake of some clever gadget or short-term return.'

In product development, in marketing and in customer relations, a collaborative vision is now regarded by GE as a way to accelerate product launches. The group also wants to use big data to unlock new customer opportunities. In its 2014 Global Innovation Barometer, testing market expectations among 3,200 executives in twenty-six countries, GE found that 70 per cent of business leaders believe big data is critical to future efficiency – but that only one in four executives feel prepared for it. In GE lexicon, big data is the ability of a company to use data science and analytics to gain strategically useful market knowledge from large and complex data sets.

'We are now actively gathering powerful content from data,' Comstock claims. 'It helps us understand how markets are developing, where to target investment, how to get the right people in place and then it converts data to operational advantage for us and our customers.'

IBM, arguably the pioneer of big data theory, talks of four 'Vs' in the use of data: volume, velocity, variety and veracity. In terms of volume, over the next five years there will be more and more big data being gathered and used by companies such as GE. It will come with greater velocity – having faster applications – and with wider variety because data will emerge in future from all manner of sources. Veracity addresses how to separate relevant from inconsequential information.

The challenge for companies such as GE and their executives is how to harness that data for competitive advantage. To make GE locomotives run more efficiently on rail networks, for example, train drivers will need to be able to access data, and manufacturers have to ensure that everything they bring to market is capable of becoming more efficient with additional data enhancements.

'Increasingly,' says Comstock, 'we are starting with building data into our product development and it ends with understanding how to take it to market. It is about marrying data and technology and marketing together. It's the difference between building something that is technically smart and knowing that customers will use and value it. If they don't, then what's the point?'

The combination of greater collaboration, leaner processes and embedding marketing specialists in product development – all bound together by sharing data – is central to what she believes will become the industrialisation of the Internet. Although online communication has been a fact of life since the late 1990s, the pace of Internet innovation continues to be driven by social, entertainment and communications connectivity. Increasingly, in the coming five years, innovation will be shared on what GE and other companies term the 'industrial Internet'. This is the idea that the next generation of Internet development will come from integrating complex physical machinery with networked sensors and software.

GE is now considering how best to connect industrial technology, analytics and customer demands in a way that secures competitive advantage from the industrial internet. Explaining the potential for GE, Comstock says: 'There is data associated with every machine that GE makes. We knew that analysing that data was going to allow us to run our equipment better and thereby deliver productivity benefits to customers. If we couple that to marketers, asking "what is the sales opportunity from all this data?" it leads to a huge productivity wave as we build the Internet into every corner of industry.'

When they carried out their own market research, GE discovered that 44 per cent of business executives questioned had never heard of the industrial internet. Of those who had done so, a sizeable minority warned that it could make it easier to replaced unskilled workers by machines and automated processes. Potentially more worrying, the 2014 barometer found that, in every industrial segment apart from IT and telecommunications, less than 30 per cent of executives said they were prepared for the way the industrialisation of the Internet could impact their businesses.

Comstock believes GE will overcome the lack of familiarity or fear factor associated with the industrial internet by making the benefits relevant on a local basis: 'You have to be ambidextrous. You have to be investing globally whilst serving local customers – it's fraught with all kinds of challenges and tensions.' The trick is to persuade customers that they will gain from GE's global scale and innovation, whilst also creating local jobs and retaining intellectual property in different countries. This marketing vision is part of a complex strategic reshaping of GE, involving the separation of GE Capital as the remaining industrial businesses seek to lift the proportion of revenues generated outside North America. Comstock claims that marketing will become even more embedded in product development, which will in turn become even more diversified across numerous territories in China, the Middle East, Africa and Latin America. The group wants to embed the enhanced role of marketing in product development and in geographic regions across each of its industrial businesses.

'At GE, we have a core belief that marketing's job is to drive value and innovation for the company,' she says. 'And we have to fight for what's coming next by utilising big data and incubating new businesses. We have to remind the company of what it is to be entrepreneurial, to be faster and have more meaningful products. Five years from now, we must make sure we fully have our heads around what data analytics can do for our customers. In short, we must drive a productivity wave and make sure that customers feel it.'

Second opinion: the analysts' view

Smarter marketing is essential for any large company. But mid-term success at GE will be determined, largely, by its ability to reduce its total 'COGS' – cost of goods sold – by 2020.

A market-led strategy will help in the long term to tailor supply to demand. But it may be hard to apply uniformly to a group as diverse as GE, where internal resistance remains an issue for the engineers and technologists who sometimes prize product innovation over market appeal.

In the near terms, analysts at Credit Suisse – and elsewhere – believe the scope for savings is considerable given that manufacturing spending at GE's 542 plants around the world accounts for $63 billion of the group's $70–75 billion COGS. Applauding GE's separate progress in cutting its $16 billion sales, general and administration cost base, Julian Mitchell at Credit Suisse says, 'We now sense an increased, and very welcome, focus on gross margins'.

The margin benefit of better marketing systems is hard to quantify. Clearly, Beth Comstock's mantra of customer intimacy and marketing relevance will be important for future product development and assembly processes. But the immediate challenge is to lower costs of production while enhancing technical innovation. One way to achieve both goals may be through the industrialisation of the Internet: using sensors, software and data analytics, all combined on a cloud-based platform, to enhance machine productivity.

GE has to convince analysts that innovation is about more than producing better products more cheaply and selling them more effectively. This is where data-led marketing could play a role, with enhanced data collection and analysis – what GE calls 'predictivity' solutions – enabling the company (potentially) to cut production downtime and operating costs.

In the nearer term, GE has to go on operating more efficiently. In its industrial businesses it must lift revenues by winning orders for turbines, aircraft engines, locomotives and healthcare equipment, for example. It must also integrate Alstom's power business following the complex transaction of 2014, to complete the sale of its appliance business to Electrolux and prepare for the separation of GE Capital – Synchrony – at the end of 2015. All this involves a degree of execution risk.

Gains from asset sales will flatter near-term margins, potentially persuading the company to exit low-margin businesses such as lighting and parts of energy management. Margins in those two sectors are significantly below the 17 per cent average enjoyed in the industrial businesses. Even if GE does make divestments, any proceeds could be offset by continued restructuring costs and intensifying competition in sectors including wind turbines, aero engines and healthcare equipment. And it has to weigh up the impact that exiting any business would have on its global sales mix. The group is already overly-dependent on the US market, even if it is the main engine of growth in some of the industries that GE serves.

GE recognises that maintaining the status quo in terms of its portfolio and strategy is not an option. So it has set course for a period of rapid change, likely to reshape the business mix and how it operates. A different approach to the entire marketing and sales effort is one part of the surgery under way. Underperforming businesses will be sold; under-utilised manufacturing systems will be refashioned. All this will be done in incremental steps, not in a 'big bang' moment. The strategic map is in place. GE now has to prove it can follow it.

Jac Nasser, BHP Billiton

....

Annual revenues: $67.2 billion
Operating profit margin: 35%
Number of employees: 123,000 FTE employees and contractors
Number of markets served: 100+
Headquarters: Melbourne and London

....

The Australian businessman became chairman of the Anglo-Australian mining and energy group in 2010, four years after joining the board. His appointment followed a period at One Equity Partners, the private equity investment arm of JPMorgan Chase, where he remains a consultant. Prior to One Equity, Nasser spent thirty-three years at Ford Motor Company, rising through the ranks of the 'Blue Oval' to become president and chief executive from 1998–2001. In his time as CEO, Ford acquired Volvo Cars and Land Rover – two assets it later sold. After leaving Ford, Nasser served on the boards of Brambles Industries and British Sky Broadcasting. The business graduate from RMIT University, Melbourne, is a non-executive director at 21st Century Fox, and a member of the international advisory board of German insurer, Allianz.

Today, the world's longest and heaviest trains will leave the remote Pilbara region for the north-west coast of Australia. Each train, stretching more than two kilometres, will pass through the scrub carrying about 30,000 tonnes of iron ore. The daily cargo is screened and blended at Port Hedland before being loaded on to ships destined for steel mills in Asia and Europe.

Far away in Chile, huge trucks climb out of the world's largest copper mine at Escondida with copper bound for customers in China, Japan, India and South Korea. At the same time, oil and gas is being pumped ashore in the Gulf of Mexico from fields named Neptune, Shenzi, Atlantis and Mad Dog. Even further north, preparatory work is continuing to develop large-scale mining of agricultural-grade potash from Saskatchewan. Back in Australia, thousands of tonnes of metallurgical coal are departing from pits in Queensland and New South Wales for blast furnaces in several industrial markets.

These are the resources that support global economic growth and development. BHP Billiton's iron ore is a vital ingredient for the steel used in housing, transport and infrastructure. Its oil and gas, copper and uranium are all critical to energy supply. Potash could also make a major contribution to increasing yields from agricultural land.

What began life 130 years ago as the Broken Hill Proprietary Company is now a global powerhouse in natural resources. Today, the company is the largest exporter of metallurgical coal, a top-three producer of iron ore, a top-four exporter of copper concentrate, the largest overseas investor in US shale and developer of the world's best undeveloped potash resource in Saskatchewan, Canada.

In the 2014 financial year, its operations, spread across twenty-six countries, generated underlying operating earnings of more than $13.4 billion on revenues of $67.2 billion. The figures reflect demand for commodities from manufacturers, utility companies, infrastructure projects and petroleum refiners – from what BHP Billiton calls its 'large long-life, low-cost upstream assets'.

Jac Nasser, chairman of the Anglo-Australian group, regards those assets as a leading indicator of global living standards.

'If you believe that global economic demand is going to continue to grow, and that living standards will continue to improve, then resources will be needed – whether it's for construction, power or products for the home, healthcare, schools, transport or infrastructure,' he says. 'More than 1.7 billion people in the next twenty years are expected to access electricity for the first time, significantly improving their living standards. We are proud to contribute to growing prosperity around the world.'

Nasser has a vision of BHP Billiton as a bedrock of sustainable growth – a vital part of the supply chain for key raw materials. He explains: 'As countries begin to develop they require a lot of steel to build the cities, infrastructure and heavy industry that support stronger economic growth. This drives demand for iron ore and metallurgical coal. Copper demand rises as they construct an energy grid and remains high in middle-income countries as consumers buy more products like air conditioners and washing machines. All developed economies use a lot of energy for transport, industry and to heat and cool people's homes. And as people's incomes increase they eat higher quality food. Agricultural productivity has to increase to meet growing demand and that's where potash comes in.'

Extracting these minerals and hydrocarbons is a challenging exercise. A year without serious injuries or fatalities is rare for any company in the natural resources industry. But Nasser and Andrew Mackenzie, chief executive of BHP Billiton, want to ensure that the company is seen as the global leader in safely and sustainably producing resources. At the start of every meeting with investors, Nasser signals that commitment by summarising BHP Billiton's latest safety statistics. He tells shareholders that he has never seen a well-run company with a poor long-term safety record. It is a vital sign of good governance: ensuring that the company has the right systems, the right training and the right operating procedures in place.

BHP Billiton's safety record has improved significantly since the turn of the century. In the 2014 financial year the company recorded no fatalities in its operations. But at the 2014 annual shareholder meeting in London, Nasser found himself offering condolences to the family and friends of a BHP employee who had tragically lost his life just the month before. He told the meeting that the incident was a reminder that the company must maintain a safe workplace for every employee.

Safety features more prominently in statements and publications by mining companies because their day-to-day operations are inherently more hazardous than those in other industries. The chairman and CEO of BHP Billiton both hail from non-mining backgrounds – Nasser from automotives, where he was formerly chief executive of Ford Motor Company, and Mackenzie from the chemicals sector. There is zero tolerance of fatalities in those industries and neither Nasser nor Mackenzie see why mining should be different. So they have thrown their weight behind plans to implement the sort of safety standards, training and monitoring at BHP Billiton that are common in advanced manufacturing companies.

Another lesson they have implemented from those industries is simplification. Companies that can reduce complexity and focus on improving operational performance will be better placed to deliver long-term shareholder returns. Amid downward pressure on commodity prices and a need to direct capital to assets delivering the largest returns, BHP Billiton has embarked on a major strategic initiative. In what it calls 'portfolio simplification', the company decided in 2014 to demerge its aluminium, manganese and nickel division, and selected coal assets – creating a separately-listed metals and mining company with assets stretching from Australia and Brazil to South Africa and Colombia.

The creation of this new company, which amounts to the biggest shake-up since BHP merged with Billiton in 2001, will enable the group to concentrate on assets in iron ore, copper, coal, petroleum and, potentially, potash. Together, those resources generated 96 per cent of the company's underlying earnings in the 2014 financial year. Mackenzie claims: 'In a single step, we will significantly increase BHP Billiton's focus on the exceptionally large resource basins that underpin its competitive advantage. We can improve our productivity further, faster and with greater certainty. We will operate more like an advanced manufacturer than a traditional resources company.'

At the same time as it pursues simplification, BHP Billiton has anticipated the slowdown in commodity markets and cut capital expenditure by 32 per cent in its 2014 financial year, with further reductions anticipated ahead. Explaining the need to cut spending, Nasser says:

'The industry saw costs escalate significantly during a boom in new project investment. With demand from emerging economies driving higher prices, we invested in delivering the additional volumes that customers needed. The imperative is now for the industry to respond to the market's price signals by focusing on productivity to get the best returns particularly from the capital already invested. That means investing only in the most attractive projects that can demonstrate returns in global commodity markets. We have to focus on what we do best.'

The new approach to capital investment forms part of the vision to improve productivity and to use new technologies to extract resources at lower cost. At BHP Billiton's Olympic Dam mine in Australia, for example, the company is researching new technology that would allow it to produce copper, uranium and precious metals at much lower cost than traditional methods. This new chemical process would allow BHP Billiton to expand production without the need to build the expensive processing facilities or new water supply system that its original growth plans entailed.

The BHP Billiton chairman is not worried that the world is about to run out of key commodities such as iron ore, copper, oil and gas: 'There is an abundance of mineral wealth around the world. There is a misconception that the world will quickly run out of certain commodities and that they're concentrated in certain geographies. That's generally untrue.'

Mackenzie points to 'crustal abundance' – the idea that the inventory of minerals in the earth's crust can sustain the world's development for generations – even centuries – to come. BHP Billiton estimates available iron ore reserves at more than 500 years' supply based on current demand, with reserves in Australia likely to last about 240 years alone. It believes there are potentially about 900 years of available potash, with significant reserves of other commodities.

When it comes to climate change, though, Nasser is clear about the critical importance of taking action: 'Science says the warming of the climate is unequivocal, that the human influence is clear and physical impacts are unavoidable. We believe that the world must pursue the twin objectives of limiting climate change and providing access to affordable energy to support development.'

Within its own operations, BHP Billiton has set an ambitious target of keeping its greenhouse gas emissions below 2006 levels while continuing to grow its production volumes – a target that can only be achieved with sustained reductions in the emissions-intensity of its business.

At a global level, Nasser argues that each nation can make policy changes to reduce its emissions, including the introduction of carbon-pricing and actions to improve energy efficiency. These policies, he says, should include measures to support the use of low emission technologies in heavy industry such as mining. Part of the problem is a lack of inter-national agreement on the right policy measures to address the impact of climate change. While the ideal solution would be an international carbon price, he is realistic that gaining global alignment is challeng-ing. In the short term he sees the development of national and regional schemes, using a variety of mechanisms, as more likely.

BHP Billiton's response to climate change reflects its commitment to being a sustainable supplier of commodities critical to the global economy. The chairman says, 'Our strategy is not static, we assess it against a constantly changing external environment – and the risks and opportunities this presents. Our corporate planning is underpinned by long-term scenario analysis. This gives us an ability to review future possibilities, taking into account a wide range of potential future uncer-tainties and systemic risk.'

However, Nasser avoids issuing a firm forecast on mid-term demand trends. He is innately cautious about making any statements that could represent a forward-looking or market-moving prediction of demand. This is part of Nasser's corporate demeanour: he is discreet and under-stated in public comments. But he can be extremely candid and forceful in private.

'It is difficult to make specific long-term predictions about resources markets,' he warns. 'While most countries' resource use follows a similar pattern as they develop, the speed with which commodity supply and demand grow are subject to several uncertainties. Predictions for global energy markets from ten years ago were all wide of the mark. Experts couldn't predict the technological innovations that allowed wide-scale shale, oil and gas production in the US. Nor could the experts predict Fukushima in Japan. Both of these events have had a significant impact on global energy markets in a very short period of time.'

The shale revolution – facilitated by advances in technology – has been promising for BHP Billiton, which is now the largest non-US investor in the US shale industry. Nasser says BHP Billiton is welcomed as an innovative investor in US states where it has shale reserves.

'We see the outlook for shale liquids and gas to be very positive for the US,' he adds. 'In many states there is a history and culture of supporting mineral and oil discovery. They have a huge advantage in terms of technology and decades of capability on the ground.'

BHP Billiton's focus on US shale demonstrates its approach to making strategic investments in key commodities – as it has done across its portfolio – enabling it to become a major supplier of natural resources. Overall demand from those markets is expected to grow in line with industrialisation and urbanisation, following a trend lasting almost fifty years across Asia.

'In the late 1970s, China took much of the inspiration for its economic liberalisation from the rapid development of tiger economies such as South Korea, Singapore, Hong Kong and Taiwan. In turn, these countries took their inspiration from Japan after it opened up to international trade in the nineteenth century,' says Nasser. 'There is no doubt that today the progress achieved in China has given hope to other nations seeking to improve living standards for their people.

'But we need to be careful not to expect the recent past to repeat itself. China's growth over the past three decades has been unique; it's a testament to the unique characteristics of China. Other developing markets such as India, Indonesia, Vietnam and sub-Saharan Africa will follow their own growth paths.'

Although size and resource ownership will remain a major

competitive advantage in the resource sector, Nasser believes the industry will continue to be competitive. He predicts a 'healthy mix' of very large companies alongside new entrepreneurial start-ups and cites the automotive industry as a useful proxy for what might happen:

'These are both old industries and there are some parallels. If you go back a hundred years, most of the auto companies haven't survived. But now you're seeing new companies from China, from Korea – even Tesla in the US – enter the market. These are companies that twenty years ago no one ever imagined would be competing on the world stage.

'In natural resources, Glencore Xstrata was a privately-held trading house twenty years ago. Vedanta was a family-owned company in India. There is always room for entrepreneurs in any sector. We take them seriously, and some will succeed.'

There are other automotive parallels at BHP Billiton, which operates fleets of super-heavy trucks to haul ore at its mines. Just as the auto industry is moving to fewer common platforms, so BHP Billiton is moving to reduce maintenance costs and increase fleet reliability by standardising its fleets of trucks, excavators and drills to one or two models in each category. And like some of the world's car-makers, the company is now experimenting with autonomous – or self-driving – vehicles to deliver safer and more efficient transport solutions.

Having been chief executive of an iconic vehicles group and now chairman of a leading natural resources company, Nasser is animated about synergies, reduced complexity and improved productivity. He is also acutely aware of the need for clarity and simplicity in corporate governance. At companies of the size and complexity of BHP Billiton, the separate roles of chairman and CEO need to contribute to effective decision making. Looking to 2020 and beyond, he regards effective partnership between the leadership structures as the most crucial internal mechanism to ensure that BHP Billiton continues to deliver value to its stakeholders: 'The interaction between board and management is the most important relationship within any public company.'

In a statement that serves as a good primer for any boardroom, he adds:

'To me, the most important person in the company is the CEO. They cast a long shadow, and are the face of the company to all employees and the guardian of its reputation among external audiences. The CEO is also a pivotal member of the board, which retains the most important decisions including senior executive appointments, strategy and the budget, major capital investments, the purchase or sale of assets and public disclosure.

'Our board, in turn, is accountable to the owners of BHP Billiton – our shareholders – for creating and delivering value through effective governance. Authority is delegated to the management team led by Andrew Mackenzie to implement our corporate purpose. That's how it works.'

As BHP Billiton contemplates a future defined by iron ore, copper, coal, petroleum and potash, it is determined to focus on those businesses promising the most attractive returns and growth. Some of that growth may come from new reserves, such as its 14,000 square kilometres of potash rights in northern Canada, or oil and gas basins near Trinidad and Tobago. Wherever the group explores for resources, its chairman says BHP Billiton will remain disciplined in deciding which commodities and in which markets to expand.

'In our industry, we operate on long lead times. The decision made in 2005 to enter the potash sector may not lead to the first sales of potash before 2020. So it is important that the board and management work together to ensure that we take our time and get the key decisions right. The consequences of decisions made today can endure for decades to come.'

Second opinion: the analysts' view

In 2015, verdicts concerning BHP Billiton's strategic direction will depend on whether South32, the new vehicle combining the commodity group's manganese, coal and silver-related metals, can be successfully demerged.

Supporters of the strategy, including analysts at Morgan Stanley, believe it will simplify the BHP structure and unlock savings worth up to $750 million. Critics such as those at RBC Capital Markets argue, 'In better times, this South32 spin-off seemed a good corporate clean-up or refocusing strategy. Increasingly we think BHP should be asking, "what do we get out of this?"'

Up to now, BHP Billiton's strength has been based partly on its diversity. Unlike Rio Tinto, it is not overly dependent on one commodity – iron ore. Unlike Glencore-Xstrata, its management is over the post-merger tensions, sharing a view about resource management rather than trying to impose a trading-house culture on a mining business.

The Anglo-Australian mining and energy giant is not about to engage reverse gear on the demerger. Instead, the world's largest diversified resources company looks likely to press ahead with a simplification strategy aimed at cutting costs, lowering capital expenditure and focusing investment on core operations.

The problem is that two parts of the remaining core operation – iron ore and oil – saw precipitous price declines in 2014 amid significant surplus capacity. Iron ore demand is tied closely to Chinese steelmaking, and any slowdown in construction and manufacturing would hurt the big mining houses. The determination of OPEC, the oil-producers' club, to maintain production despite falling prices has placed even more pressure on the oil majors.

Writing at the end of 2014, Menno Sanderse at Morgan Stanley stated:

'The petroleum business remains key. Conventional oil has generated $24 billion or 30 per cent of BHP Billiton's cumulative free cashflow since 2001. We expect it to contribute $8 billion more in the next three years ... there are early signs that the strategy of high grading, combined with relentless focus on cost and capital efficiency, is starting to pay off.'

The major risks for BHP Billiton are that the oil price continues to decline, overtaking the tumble in prices for iron ore and coal; that its US onshore oil and gas business does not deliver the expected benefits from restructuring; and that the cost-savings programme proves insufficient.

The stakes are high. The company is targeting annual gains of $4 billion by 2017, and may realise further savings from the South32 spin-off. If it meets those targets, analysts and investors will applaud the strategic rationale of the demerger. If not, the plan may be judged ill-conceived and costly.

The shrink-to-grow strategy may come under further scrutiny if a spate of mergers and acquisitions takes place elsewhere in the industry, suggesting that rivals may see benefits from getting bigger rather than smaller. A mooted Glencore offer to Rio Tinto would certainly pose a strategic threat to BHP Billiton. But such a deal looks harder to finance – at least with stock – following the decline in resource-company valuations in early 2015.

In any case, BHP Billiton would argue that its strategy is about managing its own business more efficiently rather than reacting to the strategy or potential merger moves of its rivals.

To achieve its efficiency goals, BHP Billiton needs to reduce unit costs, for example by reducing the cost of Western Australian iron ore to below $20 per metric tonne, as well as maximise the return on investment in growth projects. These include the expansion of the Olympic Dam ore mining and processing operation from less than 11 million metric tonnes per year to 22.5 million tonnes.

What is clear is that BHP Billiton, along with rivals such as Rio Tinto and Vale, is not looking to market prices to drive near-term revenue growth. Given that its key commodities are likely to be subdued for the mid-term, cost-cutting and operational efficiency will be the hallmarks of BHP Billiton's strategy as it focuses on becoming a leaner provider of the vital natural resources that drive the global economy.

Lucian Grainge, Universal Music Group

....

Total operating revenue: $5.8 billion
Operating profit margin: 14.6%
Number of employees: 7,600
Number of markets served: Record operations or licensees in
77 countries
Headquarters: Santa Monica, CA

....

Grainge joined Universal Music in 1986 to launch Polygram Music
Publishing, which became one of the top three music publishing
companies in the UK within five years. He was subsequently
appointed deputy chairman of Universal Music UK, becoming
chairman and CEO of the British business in 2001. In 2005, he was
named chairman and CEO of UMG's international operations, and
became chairman of the overall group in 2011. He has worked with
artists including ABBA, Jay-Z, Rihanna and U2, among others. Since
2012, Grainge has been a UK business ambassador, representing
the government on media and entertainment, particularly in
Los Angeles where he is based. Grainge is a non-executive board
member at Dreamworks Animation, the US film entertainment
studio, and a trustee of Northeastern University, Massachusetts.

Lucian Grainge's assistant indicates towards a sofa on the executive floor of Universal Music's headquarters and says, 'He'll be a few minutes; his meeting with Lionel Richie is running over.'

Sure enough, the grizzled crooner emerges shortly afterwards. But then Jimmy Iovine wanders along the corridor. The veteran music producer, sporting blue-tinted glasses and reverse baseball cap, has something to discuss with the chairman of Universal Music Group (UMG). It was Iovine who encouraged Universal to invest in Beats, the cult headphones and music streaming company that he launched with rapper Dr Dre.

In business terms, the rapper, the producer and the music major had a hit on their hands. In 2014, Apple acquired Beats for $3 billion, delivering a handsome return on investment for those who backed the venture. As one of the beneficiaries, UMG is re-investing the proceeds in A&R – the artist and recording operations that are the heart of the music business – as well as building the world's largest digital music catalogue, and exploring expansion into new geographic markets.

Like an orchestra conductor, Lucian Grainge endeavours to keep all the different sections of his business in tune, hitting the right notes at the right time, to ensure that UMG keeps performing. He does so from a corner office at UMG's headquarters in Santa Monica, sitting at a desk that appears to be fashioned from an aircraft wing, alternating between calls to artists and producers, email traffic to his counterparts at Vivendi – Universal's French parent company – and pressing the play button on the sort of muscular hi-fi system that features in every C-suite in the music industry.

It is a far cry from the backroom of his father's north London shop in the late 1970s, from where Grainge used a pay phone and a large collection of two-pence pieces to cold-call record labels seeking work. By chance, one day, he got through to Maurice Oberstein, chairman of CBS Records at the time. He agreed to meet the teenager and was sufficiently impressed that he hired him as a rookie talent scout.

CBS led to a job at RCA Music Publishing in 1982, then via MCA Records to Polygram, Polydor and Universal, where he was appointed chairman in 2011. Along the way, he represented artists such as the Eurythmics, signed Amy Winehouse and Keane, persuaded the Rolling Stones to switch labels and – in a business coup – acquired the bulk of EMI in 2012 to reinforce UMG's position as the world's largest music major.

Grainge's climb up the career ladder has coincided with the biggest upheaval in the music industry in its history. Since 1999, global industry revenues have almost halved from a record of $28 billion that year. Industry analysts predict revenues will struggle to reach $13 billion in 2015, affected by a combination of online piracy, falling CD sales and slowing demand for downloads. During Grainge's time in the industry formats have developed from vinyl to tapes to CDs to downloads to streaming. The turmoil has seen many smaller labels disappear altogether, along with well-known retailers. In their place, powerful new distributors have emerged, such as Apple iTunes, Vevo, Deezer and Spotify. Some artists are bypassing record labels altogether by promoting and distributing their music direct to consumers online.

Yet Universal's chairman is optimistic about the state of the industry and its future. The music industry was the first part of the entertainment sector to be disrupted by online distribution. It was the first to suffer, but it may become the first to come through the pain barrier.

'Everyone in this industry was trapped in the headlights by the perception that all the value was being lost to online file sharing and piracy,' he recalls. 'Music was particularly hard-hit because the file size made it easy to transfer. But now my belief is that the value is not being lost but substituted. Before, the value was just disappearing into the ether. Now we have an opportunity to capture it.'

His optimism rests on a fundamental change in consumption habits. For most of the twentieth century, consumers acquired music to keep. Large record collections were a source of pride, amassed over years. Today, online distribution and streaming is replacing music ownership with an access model, enabled by increasingly reliable and safe Internet subscription services.

'We are in the greatest cycle of substitution that anyone has ever seen in the entertainment world,' Grainge argues. 'Our business is shifting from ownership transactions to usage subscriptions. The per-play value for each track is smaller, of course, but total volumes of listening are far greater per subscriber on an annualised basis.'

Industry analysts share his vision of a marketplace where revenues will increasingly move to subscriptions. Credit Suisse, the investment bank, predicts that paid-for streaming services will account for $1.76 billion of total industry revenues in 2015, compared with physical CD sales of $5.8 billion; $3.7 billion for downloads; and $883 million for advertising-funded streaming. By 2020, the bank anticipates that subscription streaming will generate $11.6 billion of revenues, whilst every other form of online distribution will be flat at best. At the end of the decade, physical CD revenues are expected to be no more than $1.7 billion.

Grainge believes that UMG will navigate this upheaval successfully because it can offer access to a music catalogue of more than two million titles at marginal cost to the company. Its multi-territory rights – negotiated by UMG's music publishing business – also guarantee recurring income. Universal can negotiate from a position of strength with online distributors given its huge roster of artists – from The Beatles to Rihanna, the Beach Boys to Justin Bieber, Lana Del Rey and Lorde – and labels including EMI, Polydor, Def Jam, Deutsche Grammophon, Capitol and Virgin. As a result, the group now derives more than 40 per cent of its revenues from digital, and has signed more than 600 partnerships with Internet platforms.

In Grainge's view: 'The attraction of subscription models is that you have an ongoing measurable relationship with those consuming music. Your consumers gravitate to music as a form of entertainment because you can do multiple other tasks while listening. You can drive, you can study, you can watch, talk, you can play games. You can do almost anything whilst listening to and accessing music. It's one of the only pieces of content that allows that.

'Music will become a predictable recurring revenue stream. The days – twenty years ago – where a label had to issue a profit warning if a leading band member cut his finger will be over. We will not have to endure that again. Artists will be able to plan and see their income in a transparent way and monetise it all around the world.'

But he is far from complacent about the ease with which the decline in music sales will be reversed. Important markets such as Japan, the world's second-largest for recorded music, remain heavily geared to physical CD distribution. Others have yet to embrace digital subscription models, and many parts of the world have no tradition of paid-for online consumption, including the vast markets of China and many parts of Africa.

Universal is exploring how to build its A&R and digital distribution model in China, where it relaunched EMI China in 2014. That effort coincides with moves to explore new market opportunities in the Indian and African continent. In Africa, UMG could build on the existing market presence of Canal Plus, its TV and film sister company, which has more than a million pay-tv subscribers in nine sub-Saharan countries. Establishing a presence in such regions is vital to offset its current dependence on the US, Europe, Japan and Australia, which represent about 90 per cent of UMG's annual income.

Geographic expansion is part of a future strategy that also includes working with device manufacturers, particularly in the smartphone sector, to pre-load handsets with recorded music or provide easy access to streaming services. Unlike in the first generation of file-sharing and downloading, music is now regarded as part of the competitive advantage that device manufacturers and mobile network operators deem essential for winning and retaining customers.

The Universal chairman is platform-neutral when it comes to how music will reach audiences in future.

'Some will be accessed directly from us, some will be telecommunication bundles, some will be pre-packed on a device,' he says. 'A lot will be subscription programs like Spotify or iTunes. Our job is just to make it as easy as possible to access, and our industry has to do as many deals as possible to get our product heard.'

Given iTunes' customer base of more than 500 million in over a hundred countries or the 18 million active users on Spotify, there is a significant market potential to pursue. That market is highly geared to the so-called 'gifting calendar', with an estimated 50 million new smartphones and tablets activated in Christmas week along with 1.8 billion app downloads. The challenge for Universal and other music labels is to acquire a commercially valuable part of that customer base at a faster rate than the decline in physical CD sales. And the recorded music industry has to secure subscriptions without heavy discounting that could undermine its margins.

In 2014, the US artist Taylor Swift signalled the stakes involved when she pulled her music from the Spotify platform, complaining at the low royalties from its paid-for subscription service. Her protest highlighted the fragile economics of the new access model. To navigate such challenges, UMG – which is a minority shareholder in Spotify – must become an indispensible part of the subscription service while extracting a significant portion of the average revenue per user. It also has to help the streaming services minimise churn – the rate at which consumers switch services – by offering more and more desirable content.

The most optimistic analysts predict that streaming services will generate more than twice the revenue per consumer than from physical sales or downloads. Those forecasts are based on assumptions that streaming music services currently reach about 12 per cent of the OECD bloc population – and that penetration is likely to rise as more consumers become digitally active and more comfortable with subscription services. Analysts also believe margins should be healthy because there is a lower cost of capital involved in producing, marketing and distributing streaming services. If all this comes true, it could have a profound impact on the profitability of the labels. But to generate such profits, labels must keep discovering new artists and retain existing talent – reassuring such artists that 'majors' such as Universal remain the most effective and rewarding way to reach their fans. If the majors can deliver on that model, some analysts even predict a new golden age for recorded music and music publishing, forecasting that underlying profits by the three major label groups – Universal, Sony Music and Warner Music – could rise from $1.7 billion in 2013 to just under $4 billion in 2020.

Lucian Grainge has been around long enough not to get drawn into forward-looking statements. He prefers to stick to a fundamental truth: content is king. Whatever platforms are used for distribution, it is the quality of the content that determines the commercial returns for the producers involved. For all the complexity and various payment systems of the online world, he insists his business is about producing hits. What is changing, however, is the ease of access to such content.

'The other day, I was watching a Charles Laughton film from 1935 on Netflix. No one marketed or advertised it to me. But the combination of the lean-back experience and curation meant I was able to find it,' explains Grainge. 'The enjoyment and discovery patterns are exactly the same in music. I can play from my iPod a Buddy Holly song to my children that was recorded fifty years before they were born. We will flourish as an industry if we enable people to access and value and pay for this content.'

At the same time, he vows to invest in discovering and promoting new artists, and to license music to as many digital services as possible: 'As the market has stabilised, we've increased investment in talent and reinvigorated it with the purchase of EMI and subsequent increase in talent and people and re-launch of Virgin and Capitol.'

That investment has coincided with greater financial discipline and cost-cutting, with UMG extracting an estimated $160 million in savings by reducing back-office duplication and combining services with its acquired EMI assets.

As the musical conductor of all this change, Grainge sees a new eco-system emerging for the music industry that has wider implications for the entertainment marketplace. In the evolving media and entertainment sector, content companies will work increasingly closely with device manufacturers to embed their music, TV shows or films into next-generation products. The same applies to social networks, which have been rushing to acquire the latest online sharing services.

'We are trying to identify as many new businesses as we can where we can hardwire product and content into their offers,' says Grainge. 'I wish we'd been there with Facebook at the beginning and maybe we could have been embedded on their platform. I feel the same way about smart watches. We must be involved at the inception of these products. The concept of music built into new technology products such as watches will be increasingly viable in five years' time.'

His enthusiasm for new devices and streaming services reflects a vision of the industry in which there is more paid-for consumption of music, where music fans become more willing subscribers, and where the addressable market expands to include countries or regions largely untapped in the first era of digital distribution.

'There are going to be so many ways we can monetise music. We can bundle together music with other content on new platforms, and we can substitute poor quality pirated material with streamed or downloaded content that consumers really value.'

Those consumers, he adds, include a wider age range of music fans, in more countries listening to a wider range of artists. The Universal chairman illustrates that widening addressable market by citing his father-in-law, who likes to exercise to marching bands, while his fourteen-year-old plays Kanye West in another part of the house.

'What's changing is that we are now figuring out how to capture this enormous appetite for music across multiple platforms and on multiple devices. We can distribute in new ways and invest in new genres, reaching much wider potential audiences.'

He predicts that music companies will have a strong future if they can curate existing back-catalogues of music, whilst distributing to existing and new markets more expertly, and continuing to invest in nurturing new artists, and ensuring their music is available on all devices.

Grainge sees music companies as a strong part of the industry's future. He believes they will co-exist with and supply content to free-to-use streaming platforms, funded by advertising, as well as the market for subscription streaming, downloads, physical distributors and traditional retailing. The role of the music labels will remain to discover, market, manage the rights, curate the catalogues and oversee the music publishing operations of the best-selling artists upon which the industry depends.

From being caught in the headlights of the digital revolution, the frontman at UMG believes the music industry is poised to build stronger market positions and greater scale with an expanded portfolio of artists and repertoire. If that equation can be solved, then revenues and profit margins should rise.

'I think we're through the age of recidivism. It has been an extremely tough period, with more change than at any time before,' he concludes. 'But we're coming through it with a new model and a new outlook ahead. I'm confident because music has been around for a thousand years and will be for another thousand years.'

Second opinion: the analysts' view

As any vinyl collector will tell you, there should always be two sides to an album: one with a couple of hits that are played frequently; the other with tracks barely listened to. Likewise, there are two sides to the music industry: one investors like the sound of, and another they would rather forget.

The A-side assumes a period of favourable music industry dynamics ahead, driven by broadening digital sales, growing value from catalogue management, attractive top talent and digital scale from streaming and subscriptions. Those foreseeing a new hit parade include media analysts at Credit Suisse, who believe that paid-for subscriptions will more than compensate for the decline in digital downloads and physical sales in the years to 2020. They even predict that global revenues could recover to the sort of levels last seen in 2008.

On the B-side, analysts at Bernstein warn that, 'whilst there are long-term opportunities in streaming, Universal Music Group will continue to face challenges in recorded music'. The bear case involves a continuing decline in physical sales, the ongoing threat from piracy, the withdrawal of Apple's support for its iTunes download service (in favour of streaming) and a technology oligopoly in subscription services. Given that Spotify, the leading streaming service, has yet to break-even despite generating annual revenues of almost €750 million ($851 million), the omens are mixed.

Companies such as Universal must concentrate on securing higher penetration of subscription services, while battling the headwinds created by the physical market and the decline in download usage. They are also looking to diversify revenue streams through new partnerships with sister company Canal Plus – sharing marketing and subscription data in growth regions such as Africa – and through an alliance with advertising group Havas, which hopes to tailor marketing campaigns using data generated by UMG and its artists through the sale of music, concert tickets, merchandising, streaming, social media and radio.

Continuing growth in digital sales and music publishing should enable UMG to make a sizeable contribution to the near €10 billion ($11.2 billion) estimated annual revenues at Vivendi, its parent company. The French parent could, in turn, allocate sizeable resources to invest in music following a disposal process that has seen the company sell assets for a total of €35 billion ($39.5 billion) since 2013 – mainly to reduce borrowings, restructure its balance sheet and reward shareholders.

What is less clear is how Vivendi's new spending power will be used to help Universal navigate the digital transformation sweeping the music industry. A hit outcome depends upon Universal's continued creativity as the world leader in recorded music. To deliver it, the music company must leverage digital opportunities while maintaining a low-cost, scalable infrastructure with strong margins and cashflows. It will not be an easy melody to produce.

Lord Rothermere, Daily Mail and General Trust

Annual revenues: $2.82 billion
Operating profit margin: 17%
Number of employees: 9,600
Number of markets served: 40+ countries
Headquarters: London

Jonathan Harmsworth, the Viscount Rothermere, is the fourth member of his family to become executive chairman of Daily Mail and General Trust (DMGT). He became chairman aged twenty-nine in September 1998, succeeding his father. Since he assumed the role, DMGT has accelerated its diversification into areas including risk reinsurance, education testing services and business information for the energy, property and financial services industries. But Rothermere remains passionate about news media, having worked as a journalist at the *International Herald Tribune* in Paris and the *Daily Record* in Scotland. At DMGT, he managed operations in the Northcliffe regional business and became managing director of the *London Evening Standard*. Under his chairmanship, DMGT has divested both Northcliffe and the *Standard*, focusing its media strategy on the Mail titles and the MailOnline platform.

Only a few miles separate the headquarters of DMGT – the Daily Mail and General Trust – from Guardian Media Group. But the flagship titles of the two publishers represent the polar opposites of the newspaper industry – at least in editorial tone, political affiliation, business models and approach to regulation.

The polarity extends even to their office décor. The chief executive's office at the *Guardian* is long on minimalism, short on historical artefacts. There are numerous digital devices and a video-conferencing screen, but little else. At DMGT, the office of the executive chairman, who oversees the publishing activity, contains a library, publishing mementos, historic paintings and – dominating the room – an ornate 'Louis XV' desk complete with gold-embossed carvings. This was the desk from which Lord Northcliffe, the legendary newspaper proprietor, stamped his authority and his publishing vision on the British newspaper industry in the early decades of the twentieth century.

Jonathan Harold Esmond Vere Rothermere, the fourth Viscount Rothermere, rarely sits at his great-great uncle's desk. He prefers to oversee the strategy of DMGT from an antique wooden meeting-table in the middle of the room, another heirloom of the family that founded the *Daily Mail* in 1896.

Lord Rothermere, chairman and controlling shareholder of DMGT, admits the Mail titles have little in common with the *Guardian*. And he is barely on speaking terms with Alan Rusbridger, the out-going editor of the left-of-centre outlet. But on the future of the newspaper industry, Lord Rothermere believes there is common ground:

'I don't agree with Alan Rusbridger on many things, I have to be honest. But I suspect we both believe that the last newspapers left standing will be those that combine a very good online platform, alongside a powerful printed product, and an increasingly global presence. That's the opportunity created by the Internet. That's what we're doing, and we certainly believe we'll be around in 2020 and making good profits.'

The DMGT chairman, who inherited both the job and his title when his father – the third viscount – died suddenly in 1998, is confident in the future of his own business. But he warns that some publishing groups are in 'intensive care' and others are on 'life-support machines'. His concern follows a structural decline in advertising revenues, which have more than halved across the industry since 2003, along with weakening circulation and a shift in readership from print to the web. In mature markets, hundreds of newspapers have closed – especially those that relied on property, recruitment and classified advertising, the three ad-categories most affected by the Internet.

The survivors, he predicts, will be the titles 'that have been run by a controlling shareholder with a long-term point of view and a philosophy that supports journalism, rather than short-term corporate entities'. Those publishers that do endure, he adds, will most likely include family-owned groups such as Axel Springer of Germany, the New York Times Company, Murdoch-controlled News Corp, as well as the Scott Trust that owns the *Guardian* and *Observer*.

Lord Rothermere is passionate about newspapers. Before assuming the chairmanship in 1998, he was dispatched by his father to learn his craft as a reporter, sub-editor and junior marketing manager on the Scottish *Daily Record* and *Sunday Mail*. His fast-track apprenticeship later included a spell at the *Essex Chronicle* and then the Courier Newspapers business in Kent. He was one of the early advocates of free-distribution newspapers for city commuters, borrowing the Metro concept pioneered by another media-owning family: the Stenbecks in Sweden. The UK version of *Metro*, produced by DMGT, is now the world's highest circulation free newspaper.

Whilst he may have ink in his veins, Lord Rothermere believes that the most visionary media-owners are the risk-takers, those who experiment with new businesses, who can attract top journalistic talent, and who know when to sell rather than hold on to assets for sentimental reasons. DMGT has proved more visionary than most. It has de-risked its media operations by diversifying into a range of different businesses, including industry conferences, financial data, education services and catastrophe risk modelling. This diversification started nearly a century ago with the launch of an exhibitions business, and later when the second Viscount Rothermere, the current chairman's grandfather, supported Patrick Sergeant to launch *Euromoney*. The pace of diversification increased in the late 1990s at around the time when Lord Rothermere became chairman, as the group looked to offset the decline in print classifieds by buying and growing digital classified platforms.

When Martin Morgan became chief executive in 2008, he led a sweeping portfolio reorganisation that included the sale of DMGT's radio operations, the local newspaper business and the *Evening Standard*. The overhaul also refocused the group's exhibitions business on high-growth business events; the trade journal *Metal Bulletin* was acquired through the partly-owned Euromoney business; and DMGT's online property portals were merged with the Zoopla platform. The reorganisation continued in 2014 with the partial flotation of Zoopla and the disposal of the Evenbase online recruitment business. Over the years, the reorganisation endowed DMGT with a diversified and profitable mix of content businesses. This alternative source of revenues and profits enabled it to consider what was previously unthinkable: selling off newspapers that were once prized assets.

Northcliffe Media, the regional newspaper subsidiary including the *Chronicle* and *Courier* titles where the chairman once worked, was sold in 2012 to a newly-formed local media group in which DMGT retains a minority stake. The group also off-loaded the *Evening Standard* newspaper, exited Teletext, and sold non-core businesses from central Europe to Australia.

'The move into business to business [B2B] services created a portfolio that keeps the whole machine running,' says Lord Rothermere. 'And because many businesses are based outside the UK, we have gained expertise in growing foreign companies which will be critical as we become more global.'

The diversification benefits are clear: operating profit margins in the group's B2B operations are more than twice those in consumer media. So although the chairman remains passionate about consumer media, and newspapers in particular, he is acutely aware that business services now account for more than two-thirds of DMGT profits and more than half of group revenues.

Much of that revenue is generated in North America, where the group's catastrophe risk modelling and business information divisions are headquartered. The US market has also become the growth engine for MailOnline, the emerging 'jewel in the crown' of the consumer media operations. MailOnline's editorial formula of mass-market news, celebrity gossip and lifestyle features – often repackaged from other news outlets – has driven huge online traffic. In 2011, MailOnline overtook the *New York Times* to become the most visited English-language newspaper website in the world, with much of its audience coming from America.

The chairman compares the growth rates in B2B services and MailOnline to 'the tortoise and the hare', adding: 'The business-to-business division is a very steady thing. It is lower risk and probably will continue to grow nicely if we make the right choices. The online media business is higher risk, but if we get it right in America, the consumer media business could be twice the size it is now.'

Both the B2B assets and MailOnline form part of a strategy to deliver high rates of organic growth, to offer audiences must-have content, and to invest for the long term under the protective umbrella of DMGT's family control. 'Our ownership structure is about having long-term faith in management and an entrepreneurial approach to business. Without any fear of being taken over, it enables us to plan long-term investments. That's how we built the B2B assets and that's what we are now building at MailOnline.'

As part of that building programme, DMGT delegates decision making to divisional business leaders. Each of those leaders has the operational freedom to take calculated risks on new technologies or growth markets, as long as they meet the group's overall investment criteria. When those criteria are not met, remedial action is taken. In 2014, for example, senior management decided to delay the long-awaited launch of a new cloud-based risk modelling platform when it became clear that it required additional development work in order to satisfy clients fully. Largely, however, the portfolio operates as a well-oiled machine. This allows the chairman to devote much of his time to the business closest to his heart: the increasingly global and digital consumer media division.

The early twenty-first century has been an anxious time for media-owners. Advertising demand has been volatile; circulation has waned throughout the newspaper industry. The 2012–13 phone-hacking scandal in Britain has led to a new and disputed form of self-regulation. The reputation of tabloid journalism was badly damaged by the illegal eaves-dropping by reporters, mainly at Murdoch-owned titles the *Sun* and the now-defunct *News of the World*, of mobile voicemails of the rich and famous. The illegality was compounded by corruption of public officials – paying police officers and civil servants for stories – that heightened calls for statutory regulation.

The Mail titles, while condemning the illegal practices of their rivals, have campaigned aggressively against regulation that would under-mine Britain's press freedoms. Lord Rothermere is a strong advocate of self-regulation. Whilst the regulatory debate plays out, he has a more immediate editorial concern. The DMGT chairman is worried about the scarcity of quality reporters.

'Our biggest hurdle to growth is journalistic talent at the moment. If we could get more content of the type our readers value, we could grow MailOnline with more traffic and secure more advertising. Our problem is getting good hard-working journalists and then training them on the scale that we need, especially in foreign markets where we want to expand.'

Lord Rothermere argues that the Mail print titles and their online sib-ling are pioneers of hard-hitting, campaigning and passionate journalism.

'In America journalists tend to want a Pulitzer Prize or to go to Columbia School of Journalism because they want to do a Watergate – and that's fine, that's wonderful. But that's not necessarily mass-market news. We want to encourage journalists of all different backgrounds to come to the *Daily Mail*; we want popular journalism and we want serious journalism. We want features journalism and we want war cor-respondents; we want all of them.

'The reason is that we, along with new outlets like Vice Media and BuzzFeed, are feeding an insatiable appetite for popular journalism, and that's where Britain has a huge repository of talent. We can export that around the world. And whether we do it, or whether it's the *Guardian* or someone else, this huge online demand makes it an exciting time for journalists.'

Critics of the *Mail* are often excited by its style of journalism – for the wrong reasons. In print and online, the *Mail* is uncompromisingly libertarian, right-wing, suspicious of the state, sceptical of the European Union, wary of immigration and a flag-waver for hard-working Middle England. That tone is set by Paul Dacre, the veteran editor of the *Daily Mail*, who has held that role throughout Lord Rothermere's chairmanship.

The company's critics include some of the rich and powerful who feature regularly in the *Mail*. In 2014, they included the actor George Clooney, who mounted a furious online assault on the *Mail* after it ran an erroneous story about his bride-to-be's family. Clooney's condemnation followed similar criticism in 2013 by Labour Party leader Ed Miliband, who urged Lord Rothermere to review editorial standards following a controversial *Mail* story about the opposition politician's father.

'If you have a lot of journalists and they're turning stories around very quickly, then sometimes mistakes happen,' according to Lord Rothermere. 'In the George Clooney incident a terrible mistake happened and we didn't react quickly enough to it. And what was probably more alarming is the newspaper picked up [the story] from MailOnline. We were rightly put back in our box by George Clooney.'

The saga exposed one of the peculiarities of DMGT's media strategy. Most other newspaper publishers have fully integrated their online and print operations, sharing and cross-promoting all of their coverage in joint newsrooms. Not so the *Mail*. The print titles (the *Daily Mail*, *Mail on Sunday* and *Metro*) target a different audience from MailOnline – with readers of the physical product tending to be older, more conservative and more English.

The chairman says, 'there is a commonality of journalism' between print and digital, but he also believes in separation.

'The actual form of online news and the volume of stories and the rapidity with which they are put online has to be done by a separate entity,' he adds. 'It's hard enough to edit a daily newspaper without also asking someone to then update it on a twenty-four-hour basis and bring in news stories and run a different news operation with much more video. Online is a big opportunity and requires a different mind-set and a different editor. I'm glad we have done that because the independence of MailOnline is one of the reasons why it's so successful.'

Lord Rothermere expects the *Daily Mail* to remain the flagship media platform for some time. But he acknowledges that one day MailOnline will surpass it. It already does so in audience reach, but still lags behind in advertising revenue and profitability. He believes the inflection point to be a generation away, when the smartphone generation reaches the age at which their parents became regular newspaper readers.

The challenge for newspaper groups is one of timing. Can they sustain their print editions long enough for their online sites to build commercially-viable advertising yields or subscription revenues? The chairman, in common with many other British publishers, believes that challenge has been exacerbated in the UK by the market distortion of the BBC, the country's publicly-funded broadcaster.

'My own view is that the BBC should have a narrower remit,' he says. 'I think it's trying to be all things to everybody on all platforms. They've been weak at making tough choices because they get the "King's shilling". If you ask the vast majority of people, "do you want all this arts coverage and niche content, or would you just like to get the football for free rather than pay Sky?", I think they'd go for the football. The BBC has not been acting necessarily in the way that the people who pay the licence fee would want them to act, and that's because it is a publicly-funded organisation that is not driven by market forces.'

Faced with the dual challenge of a powerful BBC and rapidly-changing media consumption, Lord Rothermere expects DMGT to address those issues by becoming even more international, diversified and long term in its strategic planning. Internationally, he predicts that MailOnline will continue to grow in America, Canada and Australia. He also forecasts growth in India, where DMGT helped found the *Mail Today* newspaper and where it enjoys significant online traffic. Further ahead, he hints that Germany's high rate of advertising per capita might justify an investment, as could the growing Hispanic marketplace in the US.

On diversification, the chairman regards healthcare and agriculture as two areas of potential expansion for its information businesses, which are looking for data-rich international growth opportunities. Lord Rothermere also hints at further spin-offs following the partial listing of Zoopla, the property-search platform, in 2014. 'I like spinning businesses out because it's good for management focus,' he says. 'There is a limit on how many businesses a senior team can handle without becoming too bureaucratic.' He declines to name the assets that might be divested or listed in the period to 2020, however, or to predict the exact point at which MailOnline could eclipse the *Daily Mail*. For now, he insists that the controlling shareholders remain 'committed to the printed form'.

Like other family businesses, he says change must be implemented with care and a long-term horizon. Citing the track record of family trading houses such as Jardines and Richemont, the DMGT chairman argues that strategic visions are easier to implement when businesses are run by families in continuing ownership, enabling them to pursue strategies from which they rarely deviate.

'Our structure is not the only way to conduct business, of course,' he admits. 'There are many other successful forms of business which I also have a great deal of admiration for. It's just that they are not necessarily applicable to me – or to DMGT.'

Second opinion: the analysts' view

For most of the twentieth century, newspapers were the dominant form of media distribution – usurped by broadcasting only in the last twenty years before the millennium. Since then, the newspaper industry has been hit hard by advertising fragmentation, an ageing readership and entirely new forms of distribution driven by the Internet.

The test for the industry is not whether newspapers will survive. They will still be around in 2020, just as it will most likely still be possible to buy music on vinyl. But both formats will probably be of limited availability and produced mainly for aficionados. The real test will be whether newspaper franchises can successfully secure and monetise online readership, generating cash from advertising or subscriptions to re-invest in journalism. The newspaper companies best placed to make that transition are part of more diverse information businesses or owned either by families or oligarchs (sometimes both) with different criteria for investment returns.

Daily Mail and General Trust is set to be among the survivors given its ownership structure and business-to-business asset portfolio, which is a useful hedge to the media sector. If the company can arrest print advertising declines and offset falling circulation with continued online growth, then it should maintain what Credit Suisse calls an 'impressive 12 per cent margin' in its consumer media operation. But that may yet require further cost savings from headcount reduction, lower printing costs and further distribution efficiencies. If achieved, the media business could contribute usefully to group revenues exceeding £2 billion ($3 billion) in 2017, and a pre-tax profit margin of around 18 per cent.

In the years beyond, the broader existential question for newspapers is whether they can retain influence and economic relevance among audiences migrating increasingly to social networks. Emily Bell, the founder director of the Tow Centre for digital journalism at New York's Columbia University, summarised the challenge in a column for the *Guardian*, her alma mater, at the start of 2015.

'There is plenty of life in "legacy" media, like broadcast television, but it will only ever play an ancillary role now to social and distributed media,' she wrote. 'Facebook is valued at over $220bn, CBS at $27bn, this is not just a bubble or a rounding error but a reflection of how the world and advertisers behave. To remain relevant, existing media brands will have to understand technology and perpetual change in the context of cultural institutions.'

DMGT is among the few legacy media companies that have a good grasp of technology and cultural change. Given the pressures and costs involved in making that transition, its peer group may be even more exclusive by 2020.

Tadashi Yanai, Fast Retailing

Annual revenues/net sales: $11.7 billion
Operating profit margin: 10%
Number of employees: 56,143
Number of markets served: 16
Headquarters: Yamaguchi City, Yamaguchi Prefecture

The founder of Fast Retailing has been chairman, president and chief executive of the Japanese clothing group since its launch in 1984. Its flagship brand, UNIQLO, now operates more than 1,500 stores in sixteen markets around the world, becoming the world's fourth-largest retailer of own-label clothing. The graduate of Tokyo's Waseda University has assembled six other brands alongside UNIQLO: Comptoir des Cotonniers, GU, Helmut Lang, J Brand, Princesse tam.tam and Theory. At each of them, the chairman and CEO prioritises textile innovation over seasonal fast fashion. The Fast Retailing group remains headquartered in Yamaguchi Prefecture, where Yanai was born in 1949. He also serves on the board of SoftBank, the Japanese telecommunications and Internet group. In 2013, Yanai was named in *TIME* magazine's ranking of the world's 100 most influential people.

The old smelting works at 39 rue des France-Bourgeois was never intended to be a retail destination. The foundry first opened its doors in the 1860s, producing ingots from precious-metal waste from local jewellers in the Marais quarter of Paris.

Almost 150 years later, the '*Société des Cendres*' reopened as a showpiece store for UNIQLO, the Japanese clothing retailer. Today, mannequins in t-shirts and baseball caps stand either side of the restored factory chimney, rising three floors through the centre of the building. Where once metals were salvaged, smelted and polished, shelves now stock clothing designed in New York, Shanghai and Tokyo.

Tadashi Yanai regards the outlet as a symbol of his global-local strategy at Fast Retailing, the parent of UNIQLO and other fashion brands including Theory, Helmut Lang, Comptoir des Cotonniers, Princesse tam.tam, J Brand and GU. Yanai, the chairman, president and chief executive of Fast Retailing, says, 'We have an ambitious globalisation strategy, but to be successful you must adapt to local communities. We have to meet local needs, while trying to be global. Me-too stores don't make sense, especially in Europe. You have to stand out in a crowded market.'

The latest store in Paris, which opened in April 2014, is one of more than 1,500 UNIQLO outlets in sixteen markets around the world. There are hundreds more outlets selling clothes for Fast Retailing's other brands. By revenue and number of stores, the group ranks alongside rivals such as H&M, Zara and Gap as a global leader in the clothing retail sector.

Yanai has an ambitious vision for his company. By 2020, he hopes that UNIQLO will have become the world's largest retailer of private-label apparel, with 5,000 UNIQLO stores alone. Group revenues at Fast Retailing are targeted to reach 5 trillion yen – almost $50 billion – with 1 trillion yen ($8.5 billion) in operating profits. That target represents a huge increase on the financial performance achieved in the 2014 fiscal year, in which revenues jumped more than 20 per cent to 1.38 trillion yen ($11.7 billion) and operating income reached 130.4 billion yen ($1.1 billion).

But the chairman believes it is achievable. The founder and largest shareholder in Fast Retailing – who owns almost 22 per cent of the group – thinks it can be realised through a simple vision: 'Changing clothes. Changing conventional wisdom. Change the world.'

He oversees and executes that vision from the thirty-first storey of Fast Retailing's headquarters in mid-town Tokyo. From his office there, he has charged his executives with delivering stable growth at UNIQLO in Japan – home to more than 850 stores – whilst accelerating the pace of international expansion, particularly in China. At the same time, the group's smaller sister-brands are being restructured in a bid to emulate the success of their older sibling. 'We have successfully globalised with UNIQLO, but that has not yet been the case with the other brands,' says Yanai. 'I now want them to follow suit.'

As part of that strategy, Fast Retailing is implementing a twin-track approach called 'Global One' and 'Zen-in Keiei'. First, the group wants to share global best practice across each of its brands, from sourcing and purchasing to design and store expansion. The second track translates literally as 'all people with a business-owner's mind-set'. It is a mantra to encourage Fast Retailing's 30,000 staff to adopt a management mind-set, seeking and implementing efficiencies in every part of the operation. If that strategy proves successful, Yanai believes that Fast Retailing's smaller brands could each be generating revenues of a billion dollars within three years. They have been urged to target minimum operating margins of 15 per cent.

This vision of global domination is a long way from 'Ogori Shoji', the retail store opened in 1949 by Yanai's father in Ube City, Yamaguchi Prefecture. There, he watched his father expand a clothing emporium from a single outlet in southern Japan. It provided the first step on the career path for Yanai. In the summer of 1984, he opened his first Unique Clothing Warehouse – UNIQLO for short – to sell imported European and American brands.

'I was born in a country occupied by the US, so I was heavily influenced by American culture – where clothing ceased to be a mark of hierarchy or wealth or rank,' he recalls. 'In Japan, silk was often the main material in garments of the aristocracy. Cotton was for the ordinary people. But then, like America and Europe, tailored clothing became available for the general population.'

Yanai then decided that the Japanese market could sustain its own label offering high-quality, well-designed clothing, sourced from third-party suppliers. It would be sold to consumers seeking good-value casual wear. His calculated gamble in launching UNIQLO's own-label was that customers would pay for clothes combining Japanese textile expertise with the increasingly international look of sportswear and recreational apparel that shaped youth culture, initially in America and then Europe, after the Second World War.

Yanai's exposure to what he calls 'the democratisation of clothing' also persuaded him that a Japanese brand could grow internationally by providing practical, modern and quality clothing to consumers around the world. This is a model, he insists, that differentiates UNIQLO from the fast-fashion brands of H&M, Gap and Zara.

'The comparison is a source of frustration. Fast-fashion and Fast Retailing sound similar but they are two different things,' according to the chairman. 'H&M and Zara are chasing fashion; we're not. We are all about creating quintessential daily clothing.'

Yanai claims that his approach to 'clothing the world' is about technically advanced and durable apparel, whereas fast-fashion simply reflects the latest catwalk designs. To deliver on the chairman's formula, Fast Retailing employs an elite corps of 'Takumi' – skilled textile artisans – at UNIQLO offices in Shanghai, Ho Chi Minh City, Dhaka and Jakarta. The Takumi artisans ensure that what Yanai calls 'Japanese techniques' are maintained for spinning and dyeing, knitting, sewing, processing and product inspection.

'Japan's manufacturing and engineering quality owes a lot to the Asian textile industry, including crafts we learned from China, India and Korea,' Yanai explains. 'What we did historically in Japan was to cultivate those artisan skills and apply the sophisticated quality [to clothing] that is part of our national DNA.

'It is something we treasure. Look at Sony – it was the best supplier of tiny goods, such as transistors of the highest sophistication in the world. This is the background and history that we come from as manufacturers and retailers.'

Many of the country's largest industrial groups evolved out of the textile industry, including Toyota, the world's largest carmaker. Toyota began life producing looms for clothing. Other textile machinery companies and clothing-treatment businesses moved into chemicals, liquid crystal displays, film-making and water treatment.

'But the technology behind all this came from textiles,' says Yanai. 'Japan used to be the biggest textile exporter in the world, and the best and brightest people used to work in the textile business. That meant our industry had a very solid foundation in technology. We now leverage that technology to deliver superior clothing to customers.'

Technology is central to a business vision built on three core pillars at the main UNIQLO brand: planning, production and sales. Yanai claims the model is unique for a clothing retailer that sells only its own private-label apparel. Under the UNIQLO system, the planning department develops the concept products, selects the materials and designs the samples that may go into production. The Takumi specialists, who act as the gateway to production, decide whether the sample designs are of the right quality to be mass-produced at factories operated by partner-suppliers in China, Vietnam, Indonesia and Bangladesh. Finished products then pass into the sales division, where the inventory control department dispatches clothing to stores and online platforms, liaising with the marketing and sales promotion teams on how to maximise turnover.

The chairman believes this model has helped transform UNIQLO from a suburban discount retailer into a highly profitable retail brand. In fiscal 2015, UNIQLO is expected to underpin significant revenue growth and rising profits at Fast Retailing, which is projected to reach 1.6 trillion yen ($13.6 billion) and 180 billion yen ($1.5 billion), respectively. That, in turn, will help generate the cash to fund further rapid store expansion.

Much of that expansion is focused on Asia, where Fast Retailing expects a rapid rise in young, increasingly middle-class consumers to drive demand. In Greater China, including Hong Kong and Taiwan, UNIQLO is planning to open 100 new stores a year, targeting a network of about 1,000 outlets. That growth, coupled to further expansion else-where in Southeast Asia, will mean that the brand will operate more stores internationally than in Japan by 2020. Beyond Asia, the expansion will include a store-opening programme of thirty outlets a year in the US, rising to the same expansion rate as China over the medium term. In Europe, where competition with brands such as H&M and Zara is most intense, the initial goal is to open ten new outlets a year, rising to thirty as soon as possible.

Yanai has a long-term vision to fund that expansion from cash-flow. This financial discipline dates back to the opening of the first UNIQLO store in Hiroshima in the mid-1980s:

'From my younger days, ever since we started the business, we focused on cash. Back then, I was running this business with a few people, little money and even less time. We got a loan from banks to expand. But I really hated it. So, I learned the hard way. If you want to roll out a brand, you have to address the challenge of how to expand cost-effectively with the least amount of investment.'

Funding that expansion may be easier in the clothing industry because its fixed capital costs are lower than in other segments. Companies such as Fast Retailing are not exposed to the construction costs or depreciation of manufacturing plants, equipment or the property-development risk of shopping malls. Instead, both suppliers and retail developers com-pete to be part of the Fast Retailing network, either securing production contracts or driving the consumer footfall that can guarantee a lucrative return on investment.

Such arm's length arrangements are common across the cloth-ing industry. But sometimes they come at a price, particularly when brands rely on low-cost suppliers who sub-contract production to even lower-cost unregulated manufacturers. In 2013, this type of third-party outsourcing came under fire after the Rana Plaza disaster in Bangladesh. More than 1,100 workers lost their lives – many of them children – when a poorly-maintained factory building collapsed in Dhaka.

Outrage at the treatment of low-waged workers reverberated through the clothing sector, prompting compensation payments and a new accord by retailers anxious to protect their reputations. Fast Retailing signed up to the accord, even though it was not among the clothing groups that sourced any products from Rana Plaza.

'Before joining the accord, we looked at our own track record in Bangladesh and sent in Japanese construction firms to check whether the factories we relied upon were safe,' says Yanai. 'We also audited the payrolls of all the labourers and didn't find any examples of unsafe environments or extremely low wages. Because we are Japanese, we did not communicate all of this proactively. It is not our style.'

Fast Retailing escaped the controversy that affected other clothing retailers partly because of an internal monitoring system, which it introduced almost ten years before the Rana Plaza disaster. In 2004, the Japanese group began conducting twice-yearly factory inspections to examine close to 300 factories on safety standards, use of child labour and unauthorised overtime working. After each inspection, factories are graded A–E depending on whether they comply with the group's code of conduct. Factories graded E are, in Fast Retailing language, 'terminated'.

The chairman adds: 'It is very difficult for us to develop a new supplier relationship in Bangladesh because very few suppliers in this market understand what quality means. The reason why we have been successful in China is because we have been able to partner successfully with the best factory owners, who pay their labourers well, who have state-of-the-art facilities and who are very committed to quality.'

The challenge for Fast Retailing is to maintain the quality, customer appeal and financial returns of UNIQLO, whilst embedding the same standards in its smaller brands. The group's Global Brands division – comprising the lower-priced fashion outlets of GU and the more up-market stores of Theory, Helmut Lang, J Brand, Comptoir des Cotonniers and Princesse tam.tam – suffered a 4.1 billion yen ($35 million) operating loss in the 2014 fiscal year. The problems were blamed on write-downs at the J Brand jeans business and slowing profits at GU.

The chairman says a wide-ranging restructuring is underway. 'We need to emphasise the unique features of each of our affordable luxury labels, and employ Fast Retailing and UNIQLO platforms to expand these brands into individual operations worth $1 billion each.' The brands are being encouraged to share best practice in purchasing, sourcing, design and store-openings. Such synergies should deliver operating savings as the different brands in the group seek to build market share. Yanai admits that some of the non-UNIQLO brands are not performing to their potential. He hints, nevertheless, that the group will still consider acquiring additional brands that can be promoted globally.

Whilst pursuing growth opportunities among its smaller subsidiaries, Fast Retailing continues to experiment with the UNIQLO brand by opening R&D centres in several global cities and trialling new store formats. In Japan, it has forged an alliance with Bic Camera, the consumer electronics retailer, to sell clothing alongside white goods in its stores. In another experiment, the company invited residents of the Kichijoji district of Tokyo to be models for the 2014 opening of a local UNIQLO store. It has also installed anime-style signage to appeal to the local student population, many of whom are cartoon enthusiasts.

On the other side of the world, flagship stores have opened in US cities from Boston to Chicago, Philadelphia and Los Angeles. The store expansion aims to secure a larger share of an American clothing market worth an estimated $370 billion. But Fast Retailing will continue to focus more resources on China, where the clothing market is worth an estimated $310 billion, because demand there is expected to overtake the US in the mid-term.

The store-opening programme reflects improving consumer confidence in Fast Retailing's largest markets. Yanai acknowledges that demand could be disrupted by unforeseen economic upheaval, geopolitical tensions and rising protectionism. But he maintains that the group's competitive edge, focus on costs, product quality and innovative technologies will help attract growing numbers of customers to what UNIQLO calls 'LifeWear'. Under his vision for the company, clothing such as cashmere sweaters, jeans, shirts, trousers and dresses will be selling in thousands more outlets, serving many more communities, by 2020. From the Marais quarter in Paris to the Kichijoji district in Tokyo, he maintains that the combination of well-designed, high-quality clothing, produced economically, sold at reasonable prices and offered with proper customer service will help Fast Retailing deliver on its ambitious growth targets.

'We aspire to become the best company in the world at what we do,' he says. 'We want all kinds of people to talk about us in that way. That's the ambition for the brands and the company.'

Second opinion: the analysts' view

In most parts of the world, the retail industry has been characterised in recent years by intense competition, downward pressure on prices, controversies related to supply chain management and a degree of management turmoil. Yet the analysts following Fast Retailing appear united in their acclaim for the group's favourable earnings outlook and ambitious growth strategy.

Takahiro Kazahaya at Deutsche Bank in Tokyo predicts that revenues will exceed 2 trillion yen ($17 billion) in 2017, with operating profits of more than 230 billion yen ($1.9 billion). 'Supply chain improvements making use of its reinvestment capacity have steadily increased the firm's competitive advantage,' he says.

That sentiment is echoed by Toby Williams at Macquarie Research, who forecasts further growth on the back of rising sales in China, where operating margins are nearing the 15 per cent target for the group. 'After rising 65 per cent in 2014, total international store numbers are set to increase by another 30 per cent; we expect margins to rise, and currency translation to add yet more,' he adds.

Nozomi Moriya at UBS is a little more cautious, noting that the American operations are still loss-making, and 'downside risks include hasty openings of new stores in the US and Europe, profit management failures in Japan and a shift to higher price ranges among Japanese consumers'.

So far, Fast Retailing has defied the sceptics. But reaching its 2020 target of more than doubling revenues, to 5 trillion yen ($42.5 billion), and delivering a fourfold increase in operating profits, to 1 trillion yen ($8.5 billion), would be a stretch for any company. To achieve that, its flagship UNIQLO brand must remain the engine of growth, dragging along its smaller sister retail chains in its wake. The growth targets assume that consumer demand will not be affected by tax rises – such as the 2014 sales tax hike in Japan – and that meaningful savings will derive from a vertically-integrated procurement process for design, production and sales.

Given how fickle fashion can be, Fast Retailing must hope that it can continue to differentiate itself from competitors such as H&M, Zara and Gap, all of which are engaged in brutal price competition. The founder of Fast Retailing argues that it is different from the pack as a result of its focus on technology in clothing while avoiding fast-fashion changes to the basic range. That approach has certainly delivered results in Japan, where Fast Retailing comfortably outperforms its international rivals.

Replicating that success elsewhere will be a challenge, Takahiro Kazahaya warns: 'Although we anticipate earnings growth for UNIQLO International driven by store network expansion, we believe that securing profitability on a par with UNIQLO Japan will take time because it needs to strengthen its earnings structure through better sales efficiency and thorough cost management.'

Still, the company remains an exceptional retailer whose main challenge is whether it can lift double-digit margins even higher as it continues its drive for global market leadership.

Andrew Sukawaty, Inmarsat

Total operating revenue: $1.26 billion
Operating profit margin: 18.9%
Number of employees: 1,619
Number of markets served: 80 countries worldwide
Headquarters: London

After eight years as chief executive of the leading satellite operator for the maritime, defence and aviation industries, Andrew Sukawarty became chairman of the company in January 2012. His tenure has coincided with major advances in satellite connectivity, reducing the parts of the world beyond any form of communications coverage. From January 2015, Sukawarty has moved to the role of non-executive chairman. His involvement in telecommunications dates back to the early 1990s. He was CEO of NTL, the cable forerunner of Virgin Media, from 1993–96. Sukawarty then spent four years as CEO of Sprint PCS, before moving to the satellite sector. The graduate of the Universities of Wisconsin and Minnesota, is also a non-executive director of Sky plc.

In a darkened control room in north London, the vast Indian Ocean is illuminated on digital screens that span the wall. The screens are sub-divided into hundreds of hexagonal map locations, each one representing a satellite beam from 36,000 kilometres above the earth. This is the cutting edge of satellite technology, a sector that hopes to solve one of the major challenges of global connectivity. For all the world's networks, all the fibre and mobile access, large parts of the planet lie beyond reach of ordinary communications. This includes remote deserts, mountains and the oceans.

That challenge was put into stark relief on 8 March 2014, when Malaysia Airlines Flight MH370 plunged into the Indian Ocean. Long after the Boeing 777 strayed from its original flight path, it continued transmitting automatic pings – or hourly 'handshakes' – to a distant satellite. Six handshakes from MH370 were recorded by Inmarsat, the world leader in mobile satellite communications, before the aircraft finally disappeared.

Inmarsat's experts analysed the recordings logged by a ground station in Australia. They then calculated the distance between the Malaysian airliner and their satellite, measured its likely speed compared with six other Boeing 777s flying that day, and determined that the stricken flight ended in a 'southern corridor' of the Indian Ocean. The company's information helped direct the search for aircraft wreckage and the vital black box recorder.

'It was a wake-up call for the aviation industry,' says Andrew Sukawaty, chairman of Inmarsat. 'People were astounded that, in this modern connected world, a plane couldn't be tracked.'

As a result of MH370 and the separate crash of MH17 – downed by a surface-to-air missile in Ukraine in July 2014 – two safety reforms are anticipated by Inmarsat, which was first set up in 1979 as an inter-governmental organisation to provide global safety and distress communications for the maritime industry. Sukawaty predicts that international aviation standards will be introduced to prevent on-board communications from being switched-off, and that black box recordings should be routinely transmitted and stored in a data cloud.

'Millions upon millions of dollars have been spent trying to find

MH370's black box, just as they were on the Air France disaster in 2009. There was no reason for that,' he argues. 'Even with the other Malaysia Airlines crash in Ukraine, you could argue that getting to the black box should not have been the issue. With today's aircraft connectivity, you could easily transmit packets of data to the cloud, and that would enable you to tell almost immediately what happened.'

Inmarsat has an interest in such connectivity. Satellites operated by the former multilateral state-funded enterprise, which was privatised and then listed on the London stock market in 2005, support an average of 80,000 air traffic service messages every day. The volume of messages from aircraft is poised to increase dramatically with what Sukawaty calls the 'cockpit to cabin' transition. Given that more than 90 per cent of all air-travellers carry at least one mobile device on board, the company is keen to offer global high-speed broadband communications to more and more passengers.

The chairman wants to see Inmarsat extending its traditional communications customer base from the maritime and defence sectors to commercial aviation. Some forty airlines have become contract partners for Inmarsat's 'SwiftBroadband' service. In 2015, many of the 4,000 aircraft using the technology are expected to convert to the company's new GX service, which offers higher-speed data on a global basis. Sukawaty thinks the value of in-flight connectivity could be in the billions by the end of the decade:

'Today, the total market is probably worth a couple of hundred million dollars, but it's growing fast. Ten years ago, aviation was 2 per cent of our revenue; today it's about 17 per cent and it will probably be about 30 per cent in the next five years.'

Demand for in-flight communications has increased rapidly in line with consumer adoption of smartphones and tablets. That led to an agreement in 2014 between Inmarsat and British Airways to deliver high-speed mobile broadband to passenger seat-back screens and to individual devices within Europe. The satellite to provide such connectivity is expected to be launched in 2016, with Inmarsat sharing the spacecraft with another operator to reduce its deployment costs to about

$200 million. The company will also spend a further $200–250 million on a ground network to support the in-flight service.

Once fully operational, the systems have the potential to transform aircraft monitoring technology, crew applications, in-flight entertainment and cabin services. The deployment follows the success of the 'GoGo' service in the US, where passengers can use air-to-ground communications to be connected in a way that remains hard to deliver in Europe.

The company expects that underlying revenue growth in aviation and particularly the maritime sector – by far its largest business area – will broadly offset lower revenues from government users in the coming years. Of those sectors, Inmarsat's ability to meet future maritime and aviation demand will depend on the successful implementation of the largest capital investment programme in the company's history. It is spending $1.6 billion to launch and operate what it calls a new constellation of satellites. The first of three Global Xpress (GX) satellites was launched at the end of 2013, covering Europe, the Middle East, Africa and Asia.

By 2020, Inmarsat hopes to achieve annual revenues from the programme of $500 million, augmenting sales of more than $1.2 billion per year – on which it makes an operating profit margin of about 18 per cent. In 2014, however, the potential revenue stream from GX suffered a setback following the failure of a space-rocket operated by Proton, the Russian launch-company, at the Baikonur Cosmodrome in Kazakhstan. The accident came amid a spate of problems with space launches, which included the crash of the Virgin Galactic spacecraft and the un-manned rocket operated by Orbital Services Corporation.

The failed Proton launch occurred at the former Soviet launchpad from which Yuri Gagarin was propelled into space on Vostok 1 – and where Sputnik, the first orbital spacecraft, was launched.

'Proton has been the workhorse of the commercial satellite industry for years,' says Sukawaty. 'When they have a failure on any launch vehicle, they go through a period of studying what went wrong before returning to flight. We expect to catch up in 2015 once the investigation has been completed.'

Rocket failures, and the possible impact of sanctions against Russia on Proton's launch schedules, underline the significant risks associated with the satellite industry. Those risks, spanning rocket failure to space junk, drive up insurance premiums that can amount to 25 per cent of a satellite's costs. Failed launches disrupt the schedule for new communication networks and contribute to the long waiting list among satellite operators vying to get into space.

The high costs and limited slot-availability at launch stations such as Baikonur or in Guyana – located near the equator to cut the time and fuel needed to get into orbit – are encouraging new players to enter the space race. Chief among them is Elon Musk, the technology entrepreneur behind PayPal and the electric car company Tesla. Musk is the founder and chief executive of SpaceX, the Californian rival to legacy launch companies such as Proton of Russia and Europe's Arianespace. Ultimately, SpaceX has set its sights on manned missions to Mars. But its near-term fortunes depend on servicing the satellite industry.

'The commercial launch-vehicle market is going through a dramatic set of transformational changes right now, driven by the incentives that have been provided to some of the US commercial launch players led by SpaceX,' says Sukawaty. Inmarsat has signed a contract with SpaceX for two missions, hoping to take advantage of the Californian company's lower costs and reusable spacecraft. By using such launch vehicles, Sukawaty says his company has a higher vision, literally, than most other satellite operators. Its communications systems are designed to be wholly mobile, serving moving targets such as ships, planes and mobile phone users in corners of the world without reliable network coverage. The majority of satellite companies provide fixed-position services, trained on land-based dishes and towers – mainly for the pay-TV industry. And they operate at lower altitudes than Inmarsat.

'A lot of these communications satellites, most of the imaging satellites and weather satellites are in lower orbit. They want to be close to earth, because the work they do requires it,' explains Sukawaty. 'That is where the space station is. And 90 per cent of the space debris sits at that orbit – anywhere between 300 and 650 kilometres above the earth.

'But we operate in geosynchronous orbit, 36,000 kilometres away. This is where Arthur C. Clarke's theory applies: there is a balancing point between the centrifugal force that throws a body away from the Earth and its gravitational pull. Once you launch, your satellite will stay out there for fifteen to twenty years; there is very little space debris to worry about.'

From that distance, Inmarsat can beam communications from three or four satellites covering the entire planet. It currently has nine serving its different customer groups. Over the coming years, ageing craft such as Inmarsat-2 will be replaced with next-generation satellites as part of the company's fleet modernisation. Obsolete craft are not brought back to Earth – they are flown beyond Clarke's geosynchronous band. At 60,000–120,000 kilometres from the Earth, they float serenely in what Sukawaty calls the graveyard orbit.

Each operational satellite receives about 250 commands a day, most of them automated, to ensure they remain on station. If there is a flare from the sun, 'pilots' at Inmarsat's control centre may adjust the satellite panels to take advantage of extra solar power. Small movements to the satellites are made at Inmarsat's control room, where operators monitor each part of the fleet network and the map locations they serve. Standing at the wall display at Inmarsat's headquarters, Sukawaty indicates to one area off the coast of Brazil. In the hexagonal map grid, it reads 99/45, reflecting the beam number from the satellite out in space, and the number of users – in this case ships – using the communications network at that spot.

Across the digital map, hundreds of beam numbers and user-locators offer indications of economic activity. For Inmarsat, those activities focus primarily on voice, data and safety communications to three main sectors: maritime, aviation and land-based networks in hard-to-reach geographies. But the company is also a lead indicator of activities that fall outside most commercial trends: wars and natural disasters.

'What we call world events, which include the invasion of Iraq, for example, create a huge surge of demand in the satellite industry,' says Sukawaty. 'We went through five years of tremendous traffic demand in the Middle East. In conflicts, terrestrial networks tend to get knocked out, or accessed too easily, so satellites play a big role in guaranteeing secure communications.'

Inmarsat provides capacity to the US Defense Information Systems Agency and the Department of Homeland Security, as well as the State Department. With troop withdrawals from Afghanistan and Iraq, Inmarsat has seen its business affected by lower military demand, although it says its government business is refocusing on 'intelligence, special operations and federal civilian segments'.

'In recent times, defence has receded, but we're compensating by developing other commercial applications and extending our presence in emergency services,' adds Sukawaty. Hence Inmarsat saw spikes in demand following catastrophic events such as Typhoon Haiyan in the Philippines and the Szechuan earthquake in China, where satellite mobile devices became one of the few ways to co-ordinate relief efforts. The company is working with *Télécoms Sans Frontières* in refugee camps around Syria to ensure connectivity to the outside world. 'If you went back ten years, that's not the first thing you thought of doing in a humanitarian disaster. Now it is fundamental to making things work,' says the chairman.

In one example of emergency applications, the New York City Fire Department has installed eighty of Inmarsat's terminals in Manhattan since 9/11 to ensure it never again loses communications with its own crews. Still, aviation, defence and emergency services contribute a relatively modest portion of Inmarsat's overall revenues compared with its maritime connectivity. Almost 200,000 Inmarsat terminals are in use by the world's shipping vessels, ranging from supertankers to leisure boats, which generate about 60 per cent of the company's revenues from mobile satellite services.

Although the overall size of the cargo-carrying shipping fleet – the backbone of Inmarsat maritime demand – has not expanded beyond the 60,000-vessel total in recent years, the demand for communications and the use of broadband connectivity has expanded rapidly. Data communications has become increasingly important to maritime economics, enabling better engine monitoring, fuel controls and greater on-board automation.

'To spend more on communications that allow shipping companies to enhance engine controls and burn less fuel can lead to a big payback,' according to Sukawaty, who adds: 'As vessels get more sophisticated, there is also a great deal of demand from the big shipping companies to have their needs served in every part of the world. They want the same maintenance programme to work when they come into port; they want their crews to be connected all the time. Whether a ship is plying the East African coast for six months and spending the next six months in the Indian Ocean, they want the same connectivity and applications to all work seamlessly. And that is what we provide.'

Overall demand for shipping connectivity remains steady in terms of volumes, but the value per vessel from being connected is rising. In recent years, Inmarsat has added an average of 600 new subscribers per month for its higher-margin FleetBroadband service, which offers data-heavy connections for crew and operating-efficiency applications. Even so, the sluggish conditions in the broader shipping industry, combined with the volatility of defence-related satellite requirements, have forced Inmarsat to diversify its customer base. Whilst the proportion of revenues derived from shipping has remained constant for almost ten years, there has been a shift in the profile of the rest of the business from land-based systems to aviation.

As part of that diversification, Inmarsat sees significant opportunities from the fledgling commercial market for drones. As companies such as Google and Amazon experiment with using drones to deliver goods and services to remote regions, this creates a new market opportunity for the satellite communications industry.

'The drone market could be huge, including a need to provide streaming video to the remote pilots,' says Sukawaty. 'It's not just con-trolling the drones, it's about seeing what the drone is doing and how it's delivering, and that requires huge bandwidth. You can't do that with standard wireless connections. It requires a new [satellite] capability.'

That capability aims to position Inmarsat among the communications groups that are benefiting from macro-growth trends including growing device penetration, expanding mobile data traffic and cloud-based services. Those trends are expected to spur demand for satellite capacity, wider coverage and reliable operating capabilities.

If Inmarsat can meet these demands, they could unlock new business opportunities beyond maritime and aviation in areas such as education and telemedicine services. In an early indication of the changing marketplace, the company has forged a strategic collaboration with Pearson, the world's largest education and testing publisher, to deliver e-learning services to rural and isolated communities with little or no communications infrastructure. It has also signed a collaboration deal with Cisco, the US provider of Internet and data-routing systems, to ensure that Cisco's mobile telemedicine system can be made available in remote parts of the world.

This forms part of a wider push by Inmarsat into fast-growing but under-served communications markets including rural China, where it became the first international satellite communications operator to open an access station in 2014. 'We're used for a variety of different applications, everything from forestry services, oil and gas, and emergency services,' adds the chairman.

The challenge for Inmarsat will be to roll out such services in emerging markets and deliver new connectivity to the aviation industry fast enough to compensate for a slowdown in defence orders and continued uncertainty in the shipping industry. At the same time, it must continue to launch new satellites, particularly for its GX system, while avoiding further rocket failures and for a total cost that guarantees a return on investment.

Sukawaty is far from complacent about the challenges ahead, whether it's launching the next satellite from the Cosmodrome in Kazakhstan or retiring obsolete spacecraft to the graveyard orbit 60,000 kilometres from Earth. Touring the London control room, he interrupts his explanation of the corporate challenges to point to a flashing red indicator on the digital map off the coast of Brazil: 'What's this? Is there a problem with this ship?' he asks the operator.

Reassured that it is a vessel switching from one broadband connection to another, he concludes: 'We intend to remain the biggest player in the mobile satellite business. It's serving communities at sea, in the air or hard-to-reach land areas with high value communications. We were designed to serve a niche. But the niche is healthy, and it's growing.'

Second opinion: the analysts' view

When Buzz Lightyear chanted 'to infinity and beyond', the animated astronaut was referring to the sort of distance measured by time. At Inmarsat, infinity is rather closer – defined by analysts following the company as 'beyond 2030'.

By then, several new satellites will be in orbit, replacing those dispatched to the outer graveyard. These promise to deliver higher-revenue services from the Global Xpress (GX) package, which should meet demand from the faster-growth aviation and enterprise divisions. The former could see revenues rise by 45 per cent between 2015–16, according to HSBC estimates, while the latter – serving machine-to-machine communications – could deliver 22 per cent higher revenues. This would help compensate for slowing growth in the core maritime communications business, and the government market, which is closely linked to defence spending.

HSBC's Olivier Moral highlights progress in the aviation sector, noting: 'The Aviation Complementary Ground Component network program, to be dedicated to inflight broadband in Europe from 2016, has been making sound developments receiving authorisations from twenty-three countries and ground component licences from two nations already.'

He also welcomed the fact that, 'Businesswise, several commercial initiatives have been successful to meet demand for (sic) machine-to-machine, from new governments and enterprises.'

Dispatching satellites by rocket to outer-space, however, remains an inherently risky business. Competition is also intensifying in selling satellite communication services for mobile networks and hard-to-reach parts of the world. Moral cites six downside risks, any of which could jeopardise Inmarsat's growth projections and unsettle investors. These are:

'A failure when launching satellites; slowdown in client industries, especially shipping; failure on any of its Inmarsat-4 satellites; delays in the implementation of new satellites by Proton; a soft ramp-up for the Global Xpress package; further delays in the implementation of in-flight connectivity on a large scale; and a massive investment from the US Department of Defense in proprietary satellites.'

Still, such risks are not deemed so likely that analysts are downgrading forecasts. For 2016, Paul Sidney at Credit Suisse is predicting a 36 per cent rise in Inmarsat's earnings before interest and tax to $447 million, which looks healthy against revenues forecast to increase by a more modest 5.7 per cent to $1.34 billion.

The strategic shift in emphasis from maritime and particularly defence procurement to aviation and enterprise solutions will prove justified if Inmarsat can meet analyst expectations for operating profit margins to jump from 18.9 per cent in 2013 to 33.3 per cent in 2016. Further revenue and profit growth will depend on how successful the GX system is in securing new contracts, and whether rising global trade drives shipping demand or geo-political crises lead to increased defence spending. Neither is certain. The inherent risks in the satellite industry is one reason why HSBC entitled a recent analyst note about Inmarsat: 'Picture is nice, but risk should occur before opportunity.'

Ingar Skaug, J. Lauritzen and DFDS

DFDS SEAWAYS
Total operating revenue: $1.93 billion
Operating profit margin: 10%
Number of employees: 5,930
Number of markets served: 20 countries

J. LAURITZEN
Total operating revenue: $502.5 million
Operating profit margin: 2%
Number of employees: 1,354
Number of markets served: Offices in Copenhagen, China, the Philippines, Singapore, Spain and the US, operating more than 150 vessels
Headquarters: Copenhagen

The vice chairman of shipping groups J. Lauritzen and DFDS spent much of his early career at Scandinavian Airlines System (SAS). By the late 1980s, he was leading the carrier's operation in Norway. His entry to the shipping industry was borne of tragedy. In 1989, the entire senior management team of Wilhelmsen Lines, the car-transporter shipping group, was killed in a plane crash on their way to a vessel-launch ceremony. Skaug was recruited as president and CEO of Wilhelmsen, rising to become group CEO of the parent shipping company, Wilh. Wilhelmsen Holding, until October 2010. He is a board member at several shipping and maritime companies, including Bery Maritime, Miros, Petroleum Geo-Services and Berg-Hansen. He is chairman of the Center for Creative Leadership, the US executive education provider.

Every 120 days, the 61,000-tonne *Toledo* circumnavigates the Earth. From Europe, the 200-metre-long 'Ro-Ro' vessel crosses the Atlantic loaded with thousands of cars and trucks. On the eastern seaboard, vehicles roll-off for the American market; American vehicles roll-on – ready for export. The vessel then heads south through the Panama Canal to Australasia, and from there to Singapore, South Korea, Japan and back across the Pacific with a cargo of Asian models bound for the US and Europe.

The *Toledo* is not a beautiful ship. It is an ocean-going warehouse. But 'she' has pride of place outside the office of Ingar Skaug in Oslo. A scale model of the vessel was a parting gift from Wilh. Wilhelmsen, the Norwegian shipping line where Skaug was chief executive until 2010. During his twenty years at Wilhelmsen, Skaug saw the size of the fleet grow from nine ships to more than 150.

His tenure coincided with one of the most volatile periods in the global shipping industry, marked by a rollercoaster in cargo rates – a leading indicator of international trade, widespread over-capacity and sweeping consolidation among fleet operators.

'Everyone says about airlines that the way to make a small fortune is to start off with a big one,' says Skaug, who was formerly deputy chief operating officer of Scandinavian Airlines. 'But that phrase was borrowed from the shipping industry, where it really is a driving force.'

Skaug observes those forces in his role as chairman of Bery Maritime, the Norwegian shipbroker that handles more than 17 million tonnes per year of bulk cargo in fertilisers, iron ore, grain, cement and other 'dry products'. His shipping vision also reflects his position as deputy chairman at J. Lauritzen, the Danish operator of more than 150 cargo vessels, and a non-executive directorship at DFDS, the ferry and logistics company that annually transports some 5 million passengers and serves about 8,000 freight customers.

In managerial terms, Skaug's 'mixed cargo' includes the board of Petroleum Geo-Services (PGS), the Norwegian operator of sixteen off-shore seismic vessels, and even oceanography: he is a director of Miros, a specialist technology company in wave-sensors and tide monitoring.

In the quarter century since Skaug first joined Wilh. Wilhelmsen, world seaborne trade has more than doubled to over 10 billion tonnes a year, equivalent to almost 1.5 tonnes per head of population. Given that total seaborne tonnage accounts for almost 90 per cent of international trade, shipping should be a lucrative industry with predictable returns. But that theory is not matched by reality. Although overall global trade has increased year-on-year since 1990 – with the exception of short-lived declines in 1998 and 2009 – the supply of ships has continued to exceed demand. Among fleet operators, this has undermined profitability and reduced cargo rates amid a competitive fight for market share. That adverse equation is made worse by new ships being ordered at a faster rate than older vessels are scrapped, lifting the overall worldwide fleet to more than 100,000 vessels.

Figures compiled by Clarksons, the London-based shipbrokers, show more than 2,000 new tankers, bulk carriers, container ships and gas carriers being ordered or taking to the water in 2010 – even after seaborne trade slowed sharply following the 2008 economic crash. The rate of orders and deliveries continued at close to 2,000 vessels per year in 2011 and 2012, dramatically above the 700-vessel average at the turn of the century.

Although new orders fell sharply in 2013, they have picked up again in spite of worldwide over-capacity and weak cargo rates. Almost 1,500 new ships are expected to be delivered or ordered in 2015 – most of them bulk carriers where over-capacity is most acute. Several hundred new container ships are also likely to make their maiden voyages. They will include a handful of 'megaships', the floating leviathans with a capac-ity of almost 20,000 'TEUs' – twenty-foot equivalent units that represent standard-size for containers.

The challenge for the industry, which clouds its long-term vision, is how to address this imbalance: 'Everyone in our industry is at the mercy of the world economy as it ebbs and flows,' says Skaug. 'When people stop buying cars, seaborne trade declines for Ro-Ro shipping lines. When the Chinese are not importing as much coal and steel, the impact on bulk cargo is direct. The same goes for construction machinery and dry products.'

J. Lauritzen, the Danish line of which Skaug is deputy chairman, has responded to over-capacity and weak cargo rates by selling off vessels and exiting the product tanker market. It has sold off most of its refrigerated carriers to NYK of Japan and merged its on-going fleet in dry bulk and liquefied petroleum gas.

'Like many others, we suffered from excess capacity and depressed rates and paid the price for that', says Skaug. 'Now we are concentrating on the market for "handysize" vessels, which are around 20,000–30,000 tonnes and where demand is more encouraging.'

Much of that demand is driven by iron ore trade to China, accounting for almost 70 per cent of total world ore imports. J. Lauritzen estimates that China imports almost 800 million tonnes of iron ore a year, which has encouraged ship-owners to order more bulk carriers for the trade routes connecting Australia and Asia in particular.

At DFDS, where Skaug has spent more than a dozen years on the board, other macro-economic trends have impacted its performance. A slowdown in the Russian economy has impacted its Baltic Sea freight routes, while increased volumes on the North Sea have been offset by a weak pricing environment. Along with other operators, it has responded by withdrawing from unprofitable routes, cutting costs and adjusting supply to demand.

Skaug expects both DFDS and J. Lauritzen to deliver revenue and profit growth by becoming increasingly specialised, by investing in new, more efficient vessels and by avoiding parts of the market where competition is most intense.

'We have to become more focused and to learn from our mistakes,' he admits. 'But at least we don't have to compete with super-big operators that are basically killing the market.'

He is referring to the race for scale in container shipping, where two global alliances are threatening to dominate the industry. More than half of all container cargo between Asia and Europe, 47 per cent of the Atlantic crossings and almost 30 per cent of Pacific routes will be controlled by two groupings: 'Ocean Three' and '2M'. Ocean Three, operating 129 vessels, will pool the container operations of France's CMA line with China Shipping Container Lines and United Arab Shipping. The 2M alliance, comprising 185 carriers, will bring together Maersk of Denmark and Mediterranean Shipping Company, managed from land-locked Switzerland.

Although rivals warned of market distortion and anti-competitive behaviour, industry regulators approved the alliances in 2014, potentially transforming the economics of the container trade, which carries the vast amount of international manufactured goods.

'They are creating an oligopoly, and it's something for reflection – what the hell were the competition authorities thinking?' asks Skaug. 'Other operators are going to lose for sure; they are not going to be able to compete.'

The prospective dominance of the container alliances coincides with their introduction of larger and larger vessels, with capacity of 18,000 TEUs, potentially rising to 22,000.

'It doesn't cost much more to operate a 22,000-TEU vessel compared with one of 12,000. So you can be much more aggressive on the carrying cost of the 10,000–difference,' says Skaug.

Maersk appeared to acknowledge its dominant impact, telling the *Financial Times* in November 2014 that its 8.2 per cent operating margin was 8.5 percentage points above its nearest rivals – all of them loss-making. 'We would rather live with a lower margin gap and a higher average profitability,' Soren Skou, chief executive of Maersk Line, told the *FT*.

Skaug predicts a shake-up in the industry in which smaller container operators will avoid the major Europe–Asia and east–west trans-Atlantic and trans-Pacific routes in favour of operations serving ports that are either too small for the megaships of the new alliances, or by acting as feeder traffic to the major hubs:

'These big vessels are limited to a certain number of ports in the world. They need a very, very large port infrastructure. You can imagine when you get a vessel with that number of TEUs coming in – you need a huge logistical base to deal with them.'

He envisions a market reallocation in terms of route networks and port services, as different operators try to compensate for over-capacity by lowering costs and increasing efficiency. Moody's, the credit rating agency, predicts that optimising cargo routes will also coincide with operating vessels at reduced power to cut fuel costs and introducing newer, more technically-advanced vessels.

Since Skaug joined the shipping industry, bunker fuel prices have increased from $25 a tonne to more than $500. So there has been a significant incentive to develop more efficient engines, new propeller systems and alternative fuels. Ship speeds are falling from 25 knots to around 20 knots, which over a thirty-year life span can deliver major net savings to the operator.

'In the old days, the ambition of fleet operators was to be the fastest from point to point,' he recalls. 'Now that is not so important. What matters is to be predictable and reliable. So many operators have reduced speed and ordered ships built for lower speeds, which cuts fuel consumption considerably.'

Still, Skaug does not believe that will be enough to escape the boom–bust cycle of the commercial maritime industry. Instead, he has a vision for a new generation of more sustainable and lower-cost fleets. This transformation must start, he argues, with a gradual transition away from heavy fuel to liquefied natural gas. That in turn should lead to shipping that operates with zero-emission battery electric technologies of the kind being introduced in the car industry.

'When I look into the crystal ball, and I think about the projects we're working on, my dream is that we will have ships that are running on LNG on the ocean – which will reduce emissions of CO_2, nitric oxide and sulphur considerably – and then switch to battery technology near coasts and in port.'

Work is already underway in shipyards in Norway and Finland on hybrid LNG–battery electric vessels, initially for the ferry and oil services sectors. And operators are also under pressure to cut emissions, with new rules coming into force on sulphur and other pollutants in the world's so-called 'emission control areas' for shipping lanes and ports.

Of the largest shipping operators, Maersk has vowed to reduce CO_2 emissions per container that it transports by 60 per cent, thanks to larger ships and more fuel-efficient engines. By 2020, the group plans to have cut its emissions by 15 million tonnes, whilst increasing volumes by 80 per cent. But given its economies of scale and investment in new 'Triple-E' megaships, Maersk may be the exception rather than the rule.

To make a real breakthrough for other operators, more ports will have to install LNG refuelling capacity. And the price of such fuel would need to fall sharply below heavy fuel oil. DNV Maritime, the research firm, estimates that about a thousand ships would be delivered with lower-emission engines if the price of LNG became more economical. But the fuel would also need to become much more readily available in Asia, which DNV predicts will account for 40 per cent of world economic activity by 2020.

Even then, the incentive of new emission rules and potential savings from LNG may still not be enough to address the fundamental problem of excess capacity. The total commercial shipping fleet, measured in deadweight tonnage, is expected to rise by 50 per cent in the 2010–20 decade – which equates to almost 2,000 new vessels a year.

'I don't see an end to this problem of capacity, especially when ships are long-lived assets of twenty to thirty years,' warns Skaug. 'Basically, we have to live with an over-optimistic market, which is made worse by new investors pouring money into shipping and needing to recoup whatever investment they can from keeping fleets in service.

'The banks have so much at stake in shipping that they are doing whatever they can to keep some companies alive, which is just adding to the over-capacity.'

In Europe alone, bank exposure to shipping companies has been estimated by the *Financial Times* at about $450 billion.

Given this fragile model, coupled with the long timeframe in which technologies and regulations change, Skaug expects fleet operators to react in the near term by cutting costs even more aggressively and by re-purposing vessels that can no longer make a return on traditional bulk cargo. Within that scenario, bulk carriers designed for grain might switch to iron ore or coal. Car-carriers might be adapted to carry paper or heavy industrial machinery.

Vessels that are too fuel-thirsty or too small for the changing nature of global trade are likely to be laid up or scrapped. Scrappage becomes more appealing as daily earnings for many categories of vessel remain considerably below the returns that ship-owners need to break even. More than 30 million deadweight tonnes of shipping is being scrapped each year, according to researchers at Clarksons. As the economics and return-on-investment from elderly ships worsens, the brokers predict that 60 million tonnes of tanker shipping will be dismantled and scrapped by 2020, along with 90 million tonnes of bulk cargo vessels.

'A shake-up is long overdue,' says Skaug. 'There are a lot of older vessels that need to come out of the worldwide fleet. That could ease the capacity issue but only if supply and demand gets back to balance, and if we move to ships burning less fuel or less expensive fuel.'

To get the demand-supply balance to some sort of equilibrium, he predicts structural reforms will be necessary to address operating costs, as well as incentives for environmentally-friendly propulsion technologies, and a greater focus on variable expenses to protect margins. Every aspect of ship operations needs to be addressed, he adds. This even applies to better on-board technology for mapping weather systems and wave patterns.

'If you're crossing the Pacific, weather and wave tracking can enable you to plan your trip in a different way. Do you take a northerly or southerly route depending on wave conditions? Things like that can have an impact when you are operating on thin margins where a 1 per cent saving can make a real difference.'

Yet the veteran Norwegian shipping executive is sceptical, nevertheless, about the beneficial impact of shorter trading routes such as the opening up of the fabled Northwest Passage enabled by retreating sea ice: 'Even if you have a shorter route like that, and you may be burning less fuel, the weather can be so extreme that you cannot guarantee timings, especially in winter. So the option is probably only seasonal and probably unreliable anyway.'

In spite of such bleak market conditions – excess capacity, volatile cargo rates, ageing fleets and a shortage of alternative-fuel infrastructure

– Skaug remains confident that the industry will adapt and survive. It has to because there is no alternative for global trade to function. The challenge for the shipping industry is whether it can function at a profit and with lower environmental impact.

'2020 is not so far away in shipping industry terms,' he concludes. 'It will probably just be the starting point for transformation in our industry. That will require having alternative fuels available worldwide. We must utilise vessels better until the new ones arrive. And we must embed technology that delivers a better return on investment from new ships.

'This is not going to be solved quickly. It will take generations, just as it did when we went from sail to steam to oil. This will be a slow voyage.'

Second opinion: the analysts' view

Towards the end of 2014, Nils Andersen sent a chill through the shipping industry. The chief executive of AP Moller–Maersk, the world's largest container shipping line, warned of a slowdown in emerging markets, reflecting weaker Chinese demand for raw materials, and continuing sluggish growth in Europe.

The poor market conditions were reflected in the 2013 revenues of two shipping companies exposed to the vagaries of the cargo and logistics market: DFDS and J. Lauritzen. The former, northern Europe's largest integrated shipping and logistics company, saw revenues rise about 4 per cent in 2014, compared with a rise of more than 50 per cent in 2010. Sales at J. Lauritzen, with 178 vessels in the dry bulk, gas tanker and offshore services market, rose by a relatively healthy 30 per cent in 2014 – but that represented only a partial recovery from the 48.7 per cent decline in the previous year.

Ingar Skaug, a senior board member at both companies, is well aware of the challenges facing the sector. His acute sense of reality is shared by equity analysts. The industry's headwinds were summarised in 2014 by shipping analysts at SEB as a 'cyclical business with significant embedded capital intensity; uncertainty of the Russian import bans and the Ukrainian conflict; fierce competition, from peers and other transport modes; weak economic outlook; and a retained large order book [that] creates risk of prolonged weak shipping markets.'

In 2014, freight rates fell by 25–30 per cent in the bulkers market in which J. Lauritzen operates. Alexander Jost, an Oslo-based shipping analyst at SEB, nevertheless predicts that the company's operating profit margins will recover from a loss-making position in 2013 to a relatively healthy 12–13 per cent in 2014 and beyond. That turnaround reflects self-help measures including vessel sales, a refinancing for new shipbuilding and a more diversified fleet.

At DFDS, a more robust passenger market and a growing logistics business have led to more stable earnings. Henrik Blymke of SEB forecasts solid, but hardly stellar, improvements in revenue and profits. 'DFDS is considering further measures to adapt routes and shipping capacity to the new market conditions,' he adds.

Underlying market conditions are not helping either company or their competitors in the wider shipping industry. The Baltic Dry Index, which measures rates for ships carrying bulk commodities, slumped in early 2015 to its lowest level for almost thirty years. This has made surplus capacity in the shipping industry even less economical. There is no sign that excess capacity will ease markedly in the years to come, with losses, volatile fuel costs and increasing regulation likely to continue to affect the sector.

As Nils Andersen of A.P. Moller–Maersk told the *Financial Times* in November 2014: 'Any industry needs to go through a period of tough competition once in a while to make sure the old assets are forced out and that you have a reset of expectations. No tree grows to heaven, you know.'

Augie Fabela, VimpelCom

Total operating revenue: $22.5 billion
Operating profit margin: 10%
Number of employees: 57,842
Number of markets served: 17
Headquarters: Amsterdam

The chairman emeritus and founder of VimpelCom was the youngest head of any company listed on the New York stock exchange when the telecommunications services provider went public in 1996. The Stanford graduate helped build VimpelCom into the world's seventh-largest mobile network operator, focused primarily on emerging markets. He is also chairman of Aurora Cord and Cable, the privately-held US defence contractor, FinMark Strategy Partners, a financial advisory firm, and GCR Security, a private security firm. At VimpelCom, Fabela created the Beeline brand, ranked among the world's global 100 brands, and has played a key role in mergers and acquisitions. He is also a Police and Special Operations Commander of the AirOne Helicopter Search and Rescue Unit in Illinois.

As a chief in Chicago's Cook County Sheriff's Office, Augie Fabela is familiar with law enforcement. He is similarly used to adversity and risk as deputy commander of a SWAT team in Winthrop Harbor, Illinois.

Part-time police work has enabled the forty-six-year-old American entrepreneur to find a new outlet for his corporate experience in dispute resolution – or what he calls 're-alignment of interests' skills. Those skills have been called upon, more than once, thousands of miles from Chicago.

The co-founder and chairman emeritus of VimpelCom, one of the world's largest mobile network operators, has negotiated multiple resolutions at the telecommunications group that he launched in Moscow in the early 1990s. In those days, Russia was relatively lawless for anyone seeking to build a new corporation. But the absence of conventional business rules also created opportunities. In 1991, Fabela seized such an opportunity. On a visit to Moscow, he persuaded a senior scientist at MAK Vimpel, a defence contractor, that the Russian company's wireless technology had a truly capitalist application: mobile telephony.

VimpelCom, which derived its name from MAK Vimpel, had a modest beginning. Launched under old Soviet laws, it began corporate life with five base stations in Moscow, serving only a thousand handsets in order to guarantee a reliable, high quality service. Today, the New York-listed company boasts more than 220 million customers and annual revenues exceeding $22 billion, which it manages from its headquarters in Amsterdam.

'We started just as the Soviet Union was collapsing. We didn't want to buy any state assets; we didn't want to rely on the government, and we didn't want to partner with "privateers" – the predecessors of today's oligarchs,' recalls Fabela. As VimpelCom expanded rapidly in the 1990s, Fabela realised they didn't have the telecom-industry knowledge or the necessary Russian corporate influence to expand beyond Moscow. So in 1998, he turned to Telenor, the Norwegian fixed-line and mobile operator, for telecom expertise. For Russian influence, VimpelCom approached the industrial investment company Alfa Group in 2000.

Telenor today controls a 43 per cent voting stake of VimpelCom, while Alfa founder and chairman Mikhail Fridman has a 48 per cent voting stake, which is held through the Russian billionaire's telecom vehicle, L1 Telecom in London. 'We wanted to continue to grow and industrialise,' says VimpelCom's co-founder. 'We knew that to realise this company's potential we needed telecom experience. That's why we bought in Telenor. To expand in Russia, which had a lot of challenges outside Moscow, we needed a strong local Russian partner, and so we brought in Alfa Group:

'Fridman, the management and I wanted to grow globally. But we understood that we could not gain a global footprint through organic growth. The only way it was going to work was through acquisition, and that's how we ended up with such a diverse universe of companies covering half of the world's land mass.'

Through a series of complex deals, partnerships and takeovers, VimpelCom has today emerged with nine brands in seventeen countries. Of those market territories, eight are former parts of the Soviet Union – Russia, Ukraine, Georgia, Armenia, Kazakhstan, Kyrgyzstan, Tajikistan and Uzbekistan.

L1 Telecom and Telenor frequently disagreed on the pace and direction of VimpelCom's global development. Their disputes required all of Fabela's 're-alignment of interests' skills to avoid disrupting VimpelCom's ongoing operations and development. Along the way, the two shareholders turned to the courts. Tensions escalated at the end of the last decade in a bitter shareholder dispute over VimpelCom's acquisition of Wind Telecom from Eqypt's Sawiris family. The deal, led by Fabela, finally made VimpelCom a global player with assets stretching from Italy and Algeria to Pakistan and Bangladesh. But it also saddled the company with almost $20 billion of debt.

Amid recriminations between Alfa and Telenor, Fabela was the voice of the public minority shareholders in VimpelCom. He urged the two factions to not lose sight of VimpelCom's strategic goals, which he reminded them were aligned with their own shareholder interests. Explaining 're-alignment' tactics, Fabela says: 'If you look at our history, we did go through some challenges between the two major shareholders when they disagreed on where we should grow geographically. It took some time to get both on the same page.

'At the end, we got to an agreement that we had to be a global company. There was never any dispute about what we had to offer customers, which was and remains innovative, reliable and premium services.'

Despite its increased scale and market penetration, VimpelCom is not free of challenges today. It has been adversely affected by geo-political tensions in Russia and Ukraine, two of its largest markets. Russia's annex-ation of Crimea created additional complexity. In 2014, the company took a $2.1 billion impairment charge on its assets in Ukraine, where its Kyvistar brand is the market leader. Markets from Italy to Pakistan have been volatile and competitive. In the midst of their trading issues, Fabela led a complex three-year negotiation of VimpelCom's Algerian opera-tions with the country's government, concluding a deal that unlocked $4 billion of cash-flow for VimpelCom.

Such turmoil has dissuaded many European and American telecom groups from investing in markets where VimpelCom is well established.

'Emerging market risk has been a powerful disincentive to some operators,' says Fabela. 'Initially we were able to get into these markets because we weren't afraid and we were experienced in how to deal with difficult markets and how legally and successfully to overcome challenges.'

In spite of such multiple challenges, the company has managed to generate underlying operating profits of more than $8 billion a year.

If geo-political risk has been the major issue in markets where VimpelCom operates, its counterparts in the West have had to deal with a difference sort of risk: a consumer backlash over data privacy. VimpelCom brands have not faced the sort of criticism seen in North America and Europe over alleged interaction between telecommunications groups and national security agencies, which were prompted by the revelations of data capture and spying by former NSA contractor Edward Snowden.

'Where we operate, local laws on data privacy are pretty straight-forward and pretty clear to everybody,' says VimpelCom's co-founder. 'In our experience, we have not found instances where governments or agencies were trying to bypass their laws in favour of whatever it is they wanted. If anything there is, quite frankly, more transparency and clarity in these markets that we operate in than the US or Europe, because our markets are crystal clear what the rules of the game are on data privacy.'

'At the beginning and end of the day,' Fabela explains, 'we're a tele-com provider, facilitating the free flow of communication and information for our customers. Of course there are major challenges with data and network security. We've seen challenges in Pakistan and Egypt with networks being shut down by the government. We face those situations in some of the other countries that we operate in, where there may be court-ordered requests to shut down the networks for national security reasons. It's just a fact of life in working and operating in those countries, although indeed it remains a bit of a barrier for companies who are not comfortable dealing in those kinds of situations.'

Perhaps because it has faced these sorts of risks since its inception, VimpelCom appears used to the operational and market volatility that accompanies a far-flung brand portfolio. It trades as Beeline in Russia and the CIS, Wind in Italy and Canada, Djezzy in Algeria and Mobilink in Pakistan, among others.

In spite of recent geo-political upheavals, Fabela sees encourag-ing long-term growth prospects in the group's emerging markets. 'We think these countries give us a good opportunity to deliver improving results,' he says. 'We have higher growth rates in emerging markets that others don't have, particularly compared to competitors in Europe where demand is flat to negative in our industry. With the exponential growth of data services and people's demand for digital services, we are per-fectly positioned to grow these services and revenues within our existing customer base of 220 million.

'In markets such as Bangladesh where we have just launched 3G, we are delivering double-digit growth. Size-wise, of course, these terri-tories are smaller than more developed markets. But as they continue to develop, we gain much more impact. That is why, strategically, we see ourselves as an emerging market digital services company.'

This raises the obvious question about VimpelCom's presence in Italy following the acquisition of Wind. Speaking at Wind's campus headquarters on the outskirts of Rome, Fabela says: 'We wanted Italy as a centre of excellence for our future digital growth and as a platform to transfer the innovation from one of the most developed telecom markets in the world to emerging markets. We liked the idea of Italy being a feeder of expertise to our other operations.'

He also likes the idea of consolidation and predicts it will be one of the industry's defining trends over the coming five years. Following a raft of European telecoms deals, Fabela believes there will be further mergers and acquisitions in markets where it operates.

'In the longer term, we believe we are very well positioned to be a consolidator in general, probably more in emerging markets because that's really our area of expertise, but it could potentially include Europe using our Italian presence as a base.'

Fabela regards Europe as over-supplied with mobile network operators, many of them engaged in price wars or cut-throat competition. He believes that each market can sustain no more than three operators. But even that may be too much in a European Union of almost thirty countries.

'You can't have an efficient market with something like ninety operators across all the member states. In the US you have two dominant players – AT&T and Verizon – and two minor players in Sprint and T-Mobile that should definitely consolidate. Three operators makes for a very healthy market, which in the end makes the customer the winner.'

The impetus to consolidate is driven by economies of scale and the need to bundle services together. Mobile network operators have been joining forces with cable and pay-TV companies, whilst seeking to enhance their wireless broadband infrastructure to meet ever-increasing consumer demand for data. VimpelCom expects this trend to accelerate, particularly as networks are upgraded from 2G to 3G connectivity, followed by the super-fast wireless broadband world of 4G and even 5G systems.

Fabela says both the consolidation wave and the investment in new technologies – pioneered by operators in North America – are part of a wider change. Mobile operators that were born in an era of voice communications are transforming themselves into content service companies: 'The trends in our industry are all moving towards facilitating consumer lifestyles. It's about ensuring access to content and making sure that we can supply the apps that customers expect. Voice-calls, as we used to know them, have just become one app among many.'

The trick for companies such as VimpelCom is to offer digital services that customers want, and to extract a sufficient rate of return from those customers to generate the cash needed to invest and build high-speed networks. So the company is looking to the American model of content bundling, which it aims to roll out in multiple emerging markets following successful initial launches in Ukraine, Pakistan and Russia:

'The US has done a brilliant job in that transition as an industry, because they are basically selling data packages. It's completely agnostic as far as the service provider is concerned. We are providing a digital service, and you the consumer decide what to use that for, whether it's voice or WhatsApp or Facebook. We just want to give the consumer what they want, when they want, where they want it. This is the big transition in our industry. We've gone from voice calls to the consumption of social and entertainment digital services, and high-speed Internet access. Now we're going to a world that is app and digital services driven.'

VimpelCom also aims to be a player in the so-called 'internet of things', where machines use wireless networks to interact with each other to digitise services far beyond personal connectivity. Industrial applications, the delivery of social services, remote medicine, education and next-generation e-commerce will follow as consumers rely increasingly on smartphones and tablets for all forms of discourse. VimpelCom's operations in Pakistan and Bangladesh are already piloting e-education projects, and Algeria is expected to follow with the deployment of its 3G network.

'The pace of adoption is changing,' according to Fabela. 'Before there was a lag in emerging markets as they took time to follow and adapt to innovation from the West. With the penetration of wireless broadband, and the usage of all these digital services, the transformation is almost instant.'

Emerging market players such as VimpelCom have a first-mover advantage in many of the countries where they operate. That is because of long ownership of scarce spectrum – the airwaves or network frequencies used for telephony and data. Fabela regards spectrum as a limited natural resource, which makes it harder for competitors to enter the market once that wireless spectrum has been allocated. China, for example, has already allocated huge amounts of wireless spectrum to leading providers dominated by China Mobile. VimpelCom does not see a traditional market opportunity there, given the infrastructure investment required to set up a viable competing network.

'But the future is about digital services rather than infrastructure. Is there an opportunity for services to enter any market? For sure; and will we be a global provider of digital services? Of course,' says Fabela.

Given spectrum scarcity and infrastructure costs, the future of the shape of the market will be defined increasingly by two major trends. On the one hand, the mobile telephony industry will see more vertical consolidation – network operators buying each other to gain scale. On the other, there are likely to be more horizontal partnerships between telecommunications companies and content distributors such as Netflix or Spotify, alongside social media platforms led by Facebook.

This means that VimpelCom and other operators will increasingly become aggregators of online services in emerging markets. The company aims to be the mobile platform through which digital providers and users from Algiers to Moscow to Kiev access and use their services.

'In 2020, mobile network operators will look totally different from today. They might be entertainment content providers through the acquisition of cable companies or social networks; and will definitely be digital lifestyle facilitators,' predicts Fabela.

He also concedes: 'We cannot be Google, Facebook, WhatsApp or Skype all at once. But we can be a world-class digital operator and platform through which to use these services. Our ambition is to be able to deliver to the customer all the things they want in a safe, secure and convenient way. We want to become a trusted adviser and lifestyle facilitator to our customers.'

As high-speed wireless broadband becomes commonplace and as smartphones become ubiquitous, mobile network operators will find it harder to differentiate their services with exclusive handset deals or promises of greater connection speeds. Instead, the differentiator will become ease of access, user interface and the range of options for online content and services. By 2020, the so-called iPod generation – the millennials born at the turn of the century – will be expecting their mobile devices to be providing not only communications and entertainment but also a range of services from e-medicine to education. This will coincide with a move to greater predictive technologies and simplification of devices as they become more intuitive.

Fabela warns that the losers in his industry will be those operators that fail to adapt to a more customer-orientated digital service model. The business model for network operators will be to provide trusted interactivity and content that customers are willing to pay a premium for. Everything else – handsets, pricing, apps – will become increasingly commoditised. So trusted and convenient customer service will become the key differentiator.

'Network operators need to become trusted partners of their customers,' says the American who founded one of the world's leading mobile operators. 'If your service provider has figured out a way to offer things that you want and need, without bombarding you with useless stuff that's intrusive and violates privacy, then that has real value.

'In this industry, you always talk about how to define different parts of the marketplace. The ultimate place to be in the mobile market is to be a trusted adviser and lifestyle facilitator to individual customers. We must personalise what people want, with bespoke services. It will not be easy to get there, but that must be our aspiration and ambition: a bespoke provider to a segment of one, anticipating and meeting our customers' needs. This will be the future of our industry.'

Second opinion: the analysts' view

Companies tend to face a 'perfect storm' infrequently. Recent sufferers include the UK's City Link (collapsed) and Tesco (allegations of fraud and over-stated profits); France's Alstom (break-up and record Department of Justice fines); Malaysian Airlines (crashes and state intervention); and possibly VimpelCom.

The telecommunications group, serving several hundred million customers in more than a dozen countries, cut its dividend by more than 50 per cent in early 2014 to lower its debt. Analysts argued that it had under-invested in its Russian network infrastructure; the devaluation of the rouble hit the company's dollar-reported numbers; its Ukrainian business faced major uncertainty; and the chief executive of Telenor, its second-largest shareholder, resigned from the board amid media allegations of corrupt practices.

These issues coincided with continued pressure on average revenues per user, pressure for consolidation across the industry and high debts. As Ivan Kim, sector analyst at VTB Capital, noted in autumn 2014:

'The fundamental outlook remains bleak for now. Depreciation of currencies in all key markets coupled with subdued growth expectations amount to an unexciting earnings outlook.... Consolidation in Italy could change the investment case completely but is uncertain.'

On the plus side, VimpelCom is well placed in emerging markets and has made some progress in turning around its operations in Russia, where networks are being upgraded. The management reportedly believes that synergies exceeding $2.5 billion can be extracted from the Wind merger. And financial cost controls have led to improved underlying margins. The company's reliance on Russia for about 37 per cent of profits and on Italy for 29 per cent of earnings should deliver good growth exposure when, or more likely if, those markets recover.

So the business remains well placed to benefit from growing demand for data services and wireless-broadband content in emerging markets. Before the rouble collapse, analysts were predicting fairly stable revenues of $20–21 billion each year to 2017, with earnings before interest, tax, depreciation and amortisation of about $8.2 billion. On a constant currency basis, it might get there. But volatile exchange rates are testament to emerging market risk. In good times, telecom companies such as VimpelCom can outperform larger and more mature market operators. But such times have been in short supply since the financial crisis. Even industry giants such as AT&T and Vodafone have diversified horizontally – into content and cable – to offset squeezed margins in the mobile market.

Such convergence has gathered pace in early 2015 with BT's planned acquisition of mobile network EE and the offer by Hutchison Whampoa for O2. This consolidation, albeit in mature markets such as the UK, could put further pressure on smaller players to join the merger activity.

The business fundamentals in telecommunications remain sound: continued overall subscriber growth and a transition from cheap voice to richer data services. But the journey to a more stable higher-margin business looks fraught, especially in countries suffering political and economic tension.

Emma Marcegaglia, Eni and BusinessEurope

ENI
Annual revenues: $135.7 billion
Operating profit margin: 7.7%
Number of employees: 82,300
Number of markets served: 85
Headquarters: Rome

MARCEGAGLIA
Annual revenues: $4.76 billion
Operating profit margin: N/A
Number of employees: 7,000
Number of markets served: 17 countries
Headquarters: Mantova

One of Italy's leading businesswomen, Marcegaglia spent twelve years in a variety of roles at Confindustria before becoming president of the Italian employers' confederation in 2008. During her presidency, until May 2012, she was also a member of the management board at Banco Popolare and

a director of FinecoBank. In 2013, she was named president
of BusinessEurope, the regional organisation for employers'
organisations, and became non-executive chairman of Eni, the
Italian oil and gas major. Marcegaglia, a graduate of Bocconi
University in Milan and New York University, is deputy chairman and
joint chief executive of Marcegaglia, the family-controlled speciality
steels business. She is also a non-executive board member at
Bracco, the Italian healthcare company, and Italcementi, the
country's building products group.

Most business leaders 'go plural' in the sunset of their careers. Having climbed the corporate ladder in one industry, chairmen and chief executives often channel their expertise in part-time boardroom roles on company boards or trade associations as they near retirement. By then, the plural life is less competitive; less of a marathon.

Emma Marcegaglia defies that stereotype. The Italian businesswoman went plural early in her career, motivated by a competitive streak that turned her into a corporate tri-athlete. In three different roles, she worries constantly about competitiveness and whether the groups she leads are fit to succeed in their respective markets.

As president of BusinessEurope, Marcegaglia agitates about competition and structural reform – or Europe's lack of it – on behalf of employers' organisations from thirty-five countries. She is equally concerned about energy costs, trade barriers, skills shortages, sluggish investment and the bureaucracy facing an industrial sector that employs more than 30 million people in Europe. Such trends also worry Marcegaglia in her role as board chairman at Eni, Italy's largest integrated energy company – and the country's largest industrial group as a whole, by market capitalisation. And global competitiveness is a constant issue at Marcegaglia SpA, where she is co-chief executive with her brother Antonio of a family-controlled group that is the world's leading steel processor.

Her three-way career means Marcegaglia is, at one and the same time, portraying the public face of a business association demanding action to restore European industrial competitiveness, whilst also overseeing one of the world's top twenty energy companies – producing more than 1.56 million barrels of oil and gas-equivalent a day – and jointly managing a family business with a daily output of some 5,500 kilometres of steel products.

In all three roles, Marcegaglia says she is pushing a reform agenda: 'We are constantly adapting to risks in each area. At the family company, the decision-making process to manage risk is very fast and easy. At Eni, the CEO manages the company, but almost all important decisions come to the board – where the chairman has ultimate responsibility for creating long-term value for shareholders. At BusinessEurope, I have to be vocal and speak up about competitiveness in a very clear way, warning of the risks if politicians or the European Commission fails to act.'

Asked if she might be described as a progressive troublemaker, Marcegaglia laughs. 'Yes, I like that.' But the trouble with Europe, she warns, is that progress is too slow in coming. The risks of industrial stagnation are rising in a global marketplace where other regions or countries enjoy significantly higher growth.

Marcegaglia hopes the European Commission of Jean-Claude Juncker, serving from 2014 to 2019, will prove more supportive of industry than the previous cohort of commissioners.

'There has been a kind of frustration in the business community because the previous Commission said loudly that one of their aims was to lift the proportion of GDP coming from industry to 20 per cent in 2020, but they did not follow up this target with concrete action,' says the president of BusinessEurope. 'We need better governance and organisation from the Commission, and a cluster of expertise that avoids contradictory policy positions, especially on energy and competitiveness.'

She applauds the composition of the Commission appointed in 2014, in which the portfolios of climate action and energy have been combined. A single commissioner has also been appointed to oversee jobs, growth, investment and competitiveness.

But Marcegaglia warns that Europe must take action to repair the damage caused by a lack of growth and structural reform just to catch up with rival trading blocs. Only then can Europe hope for a sustained recovery. Europe has stagnated, she believes, because it is handicapped by high operating costs, excessive energy prices and too much red tape. Since the financial crisis and great recession of 2008–09, this has contributed to disinvestment and eroding competitiveness – reflected by the loss of 6 million jobs across the EU. In the first twelve years of the twenty-first century, Europe also saw its share of worldwide foreign direct investment fall from 40 to 24 per cent. Over the same period, industrial gas prices have fallen four-fold in the US compared with Europe. Electricity prices in the EU are more than double those of the US and Russia, and 20 per cent higher than in China.

Given her own exposure to energy costs as joint-CEO of the Marcegaglia steel company and as chairman of Eni, Marcegaglia believes that Europe must find alternative and more dependable sources of energy. This, in turn, may require a rethink on the EU's target to cut greenhouse gas emissions by 40 per cent by 2030. A rethink is necessary to ensure that European industry is not disadvantaged in relation to competitors not facing such swingeing changes: 'This target must be adjusted. To unilaterally cut emissions by 40 per cent without reciprocal action when our energy costs are very high and security of supply is uncertain clearly puts European industry at a disadvantage,' she argues.

A more coherent European policy framework on energy and climate change is one of ten priorities for BusinessEurope as part of its vision to boost investment, growth and employment. That vision requires action, according to Marcegaglia, to improve access to finance for companies, to further develop the single market – particularly in the digital economy; to see better and more coherent regulation; to modernise labour markets, education and training; to invest more in research and development; to improve governance at the European Commission; to prioritise investment in national budgets; and to secure trade agreements that will enhance access to worldwide markets. Such action is vital, in her view, for Europe to strengthen its industrial base.

In addition to energy costs, Marcegaglia fears that her ambition for a resurgent European industrial sector could be jeopardised by a combination of bureaucracy and the absence of trade agreements with major economic powers such as the US and Japan.

'Red tape in Europe is still very bad,' she points out. 'The cost of doing business in the EU is still very high, mainly due to the fact that the internal market has not been completed and different member states do not co-ordinate regulation or policy implementation.'

Given the challenges facing Europe, Marcegaglia says she is a pessimist in the short term about recovery prospects. But long term she is optimistic that the lack of alternatives will lead eventually to structural reform and a more coherent European industrial policy. Of the ten priority areas for European growth and investment, she rates international trade as the issue most likely to see progress.

'In the end I am optimistic about this, although there are major hurdles to overcome, because the cost of not having an agreement with the US would be extremely damaging – the situation in Europe would be even worse than it is today.'

Similarly, the societal and political costs of persistently high unemployment – especially among the young – alongside unsustainable public finances, potential deflation and geo-political tensions are likely, eventually, to lead to structural reforms across Europe. She just regrets that Europe tends to take action only after all the alternatives have been exhausted, rather than as proactive policy.

At Eni and Marcegaglia SpA, the two companies that constitute the other parts of her triangular business life, she insists that the reform agenda is being driven by market opportunity and entrepreneurialism, and not the sort of defensiveness seen at the EU regional level. Eni, in which the Italian state has a 30 per cent stake, has embarked on a restructuring to focus on its exploration and production operations, whilst reducing its exposure to unprofitable refining operations. 'We are restructuring every part of our refinery business, as well as the chemicals operations and gas distribution,' says the chairman.

The overhaul will increase the group's upstream emphasis, whereby it invests in seeking and extracting new oil finds. Eni's renewed focus follows a re-organisation of its gas, power, refining and marketing operations, in which Eni has renegotiated supply contracts, cut transport capacity and reduced refining capacity by more than 50 per cent since 2012.

In parallel, Eni has continued to spend on exploration, discovering more than 9.5 billion barrels of oil equivalent in the five years up to 2013. Those discoveries have followed significant investments in the Gulf of Mexico, Indonesia and sub-Saharan Africa. As Marcegaglia put it: 'We have made more discoveries than any other oil and gas company in the world in recent years, giving us a lot of reserves that we can work.' She

hopes the new reserves will generate cash over time for further investment and shareholder returns at Eni, the world's seventeenth-largest oil
and gas explorer.

Oil exploration in parts of the world with untapped reserves can
be a risky business. Finding new discoveries is hazardous, costly and
complex. And there is a reputational threat if securing those reserves
prompts questions of unethical transactions or corruption. In 2014, Eni
chief executive Claudio Descalzi was placed under investigation by pros-
ecutors in Milan over the acquisition of offshore oil blocs in Nigeria in
2011. The company has denied any wrongdoing.

Marcegaglia makes no comment about the specifics of the case. But
she insists that Eni is among the best oil majors when it comes to transparency, compliance and ethical standards.

'The CEO manages the company, but the board has a major role in
decision making and ensuring compliance standards are met,' she adds.
'At Eni, a decision on upstream investments of more than 300 million
euros [$340 million] comes before the board – which means 99 per cent
of all investment. We are, as independent directors, working a lot on
better procedures for audit controls, on anti-corruption measures, and
on embedding sustainability into all our processes for decision making.'

She maintains that the focus on compliance will not divert Eni from
realising its long-term vision of becoming an upstream oil and gas company seeking long-term returns from operations in ninety countries,
where it employs more than 80,000 people. 'We have to be long-term
because when you start an exploration, it may be ten years before production begins – that's the nature of the business,' she says.

Her emphasis on long-term returns also reflects the vision of the
eponymous family company where Marcegaglia shares power with
her brother, who serves as both chairman and joint-CEO. The company, founded in 1959 by their father Steno Marcegaglia, has expanded
from a manufacturer of irrigation pipes through a series of acquisitions, over two generations, into an international group with forty-three
plants producing stainless steel pipes, scaffolding, crash barriers, tubes
and bars.

Dozens of acquisitions since the early 1960s paved the way for a privately-held group with twenty-two steel-processing centres in Italy, the UK, Russia, Brazil, China and the US. The family business, generating revenues of about €5 billion ($5.8 billion) a year, provides more than 5 million tonnes of steel products to the construction, property development, automotive and food and dairy industries.

Marcegaglia says the long-term family shareholding and unified vision of the family-led management team allows for extremely fast decision making and an ability to adjust output to demand quickly. It also allows for opportunistic acquisitions or takeover bids, partly to take advantage of depressed valuations in a steel industry handicapped by widespread over-capacity.

Just as she is driving a reform agenda at BusinessEurope and Eni, the joint chief executive of Marcegaglia SpA says that the family-owned business could take radical steps to ensure its long-term competitiveness:

'The over-capacity in our industry is going to stay for a while, so we are considering how to work with other companies and to consider alternative structures. Some years ago, the idea of a merger or to bring in investment funds or to raise equity would have been difficult to accept for a family-owned company. But it's even more important to be stronger and competitive in our arena.'

Marcegaglia declines to speculate on what a new ownership structure might look like for the family company, or what sort of partnerships it might lead to. But as an example of potential co-operation, she points to the group's joint bid with ArcelorMittal, the French-Indian steelmaker, for Ilva (the Italian plant that is Europe's largest-capacity steel factory) as a potential sign of things to come:

'We are considering a range of options because the situation has changed completely since 2007 and 2008. It seems another century. So we have to think about how to be very efficient and how to work with other companies such as ArcelorMittal, and if this makes us more solid and stronger and competitive, that's fine.'

The willingness to consider a fundamental change to the family's ownership structure – with the Marcegaglias likely to retain majority control in a potential alliance or cross-holding partnership – is part of her reform-minded approach to business in general. 'If you are unwilling to change; if you stay closed – that's a weakness,' she says.

A vision of reducing excess capacity, of consolidating where it makes sense and becoming more competitive on a global basis is a common theme at not only the family steel company, but also Eni and BusinessEurope. The businesswoman whose interests straddle all three believes that competitiveness requires more innovation, a flexible approach to finance and investment, and a more entrepreneurial mindset.

If those reforms could lift EU growth from an anaemic 1–2 per cent to 3 per cent by 2020, BusinessEurope estimates it could create 1.4 million jobs. The group's president believes that free-trade agreements with the US and Japan could be pivotal in unlocking that growth. But it will also require the sort of structural labour market reforms that are finally being introduced in Spain and Italy. Such reforms will bring these markets closer to the sort of liberalised labour regimes of the UK and the US. But it could take decades before established working practices and regulations really change in practice.

Those reforms will not solve Europe's competitiveness-deficit in isolation, however. Marcegaglia reiterates that it will require a solution to the cost of energy and supply-security. She believes that there should be more investment in data-driven innovation, improved 'industrial governance' to cut red tape, and a renewed focus on education, training and work-based learning. And all of that must be implemented, she says, within a European single market that functions coherently.

'Europe has to change the way that its institutions and national governments look at competition. Europe is still too risk averse, especially compared to the US,' Marcegaglia, who spent some of her formative student years in the US, argues. 'The big difference between attitudes in Europe and the US is that the EU is too cautious. In the US you can innovate, you can take risks and it's OK to fail. In Europe, the aversion to risk, combined with regulation, social costs and attitudes to wealth creation, acts as a deterrent. Without a solution to this, I think, everything goes downhill.'

Second opinion: the analysts' view

Companies are not expecting much help from policymakers in the near-term regarding the issues that irritate them: relatively high cost of energy, absence of global free trade agreements and the burden of red tape.

Business groups will continue to agitate for fundamental reform. But companies are implementing self-help measures (code for cost-cutting) and global expansion plans amid expectations that markets will remain difficult for some time to come.

In two sectors highly exposed to commodity pricing – oil and steel-making – trading conditions have been hampered by surplus supply and volatile demand. The situation is particularly acute for Eni, which was hit by the 2014 collapse in oil prices. Still, the company is cutting its refining capacity and concentrating on exploration; analysts at UBS describe exploration as a 'favoured place for oil companies to seek short-term cost cuts'. Jon Rigby at UBS adds, 'The investment case for Eni relies on strong organically driven upstream growth and restructuring of the remaining businesses.'

But Deutsche Bank is more cautious. Lucas Herrmann, market researcher at Deutsche, warns of uncertainties surrounding 'the shape and timing of any recovery', adding that it is therefore 'too early to turn outright positive on the sector' given the pricing environment, the costs of exploration and the operational challenge of extracting new reserves from hard-to-reach places.

Steel prices have been equally volatile, but Marcegaglia is somewhat protected from the worst of the commodities environment by its speciality focus in the industry. The pressure on prices, however, is likely to remain given OECD forecasts that world steel production capacity could grow by almost 200 metric tonnes, or 9 per cent, between 2013 and 2017.

The speciality steel business has out-performed the much larger market for carbon steels, with shipments growing at almost 8 per cent a year compared with about 5 per cent for steel bars, flat-rolled products, plate and structural steel. The stainless segment also has relatively low inventories, implying a fairly tight grip on costs.

There is no room for complacency. Market competition and the pricing environment are brutal, and the cost implications of a European manufacturing base remain high. It will require artful management to secure policy reforms that genuinely enhance business prospects, particularly when European governments appear to have little interest in tax concessions or investment incentives, and when globalisation poses additional pressures. Given those challenges, management at Eni and Marcegaglia have their work cut out. Perhaps the only consolation is that barriers to entry are high. It is hard for new competitors to challenge companies with either long-held production assets or tight customer relationships for specialist products. But the woman playing a leading role at both companies takes nothing for granted. Reform remains high on her agenda. The relative performance of European companies, compared with American and Asian rivals, suggests it needs to be.

CONCLUSION

Business has an image problem. For generations, arguably throughout industrial history, corporate reputations have waned in periods of austerity and economic malaise. When consumer confidence and growth prospects are low, companies face disproportionate criticism for any strategic mis-step or earnings disappointment. At such times, large companies and the individuals who lead them are portrayed frequently as self-serving and driven by wealth-creation for the few rather than serving the interests of the many – notably their employees and consumers.

Anti-corporate rhetoric intensifies with every major crisis – the Wall Street Crash of 1929 and the ensuing Great Depression; post-war austerity; the oil price shocks of the 1970s; and the Great Recession induced by the 2008–09 debt calamity. In slowing economies, the over-riding sentiment towards commercial enterprise is often hostile in political speeches, newspaper editorials, regulatory rulings, academic works and online chatter. The indictments follow a similar pattern. Among recent charges, banks are accused of gauging their customers. Oil and gas companies are criticised for depleting resources and exacerbating climate change. Manufacturers risk condemnation by outsourcing jobs to low-cost countries, where employee rights may be compromised. Product safety, it is supposed, has been relegated behind the search for savings and global scale. In the technology and online world, commerce appears to be dominated by a new elite of super-rich mainly US and Chinese oligarchs. Retailers are condemned for allegedly mistreating suppliers, scrimping on workers' pay or fleecing their customers. Passengers laugh ironically at the service promises of airlines and rail operators. Providers of healthcare, education and welfare services risk public ire if they are seen to be profiteering, especially in countries where social welfare is state-funded.

In this censorious climate, generous executive pay is bad; restraint is good. Financial discipline is lauded; opportunistic takeovers are questioned. The populist criticism is fuelled and amplified by a news media industry that fears for its own future.

Given this backdrop, many business leaders are reluctant to speak out. They fear opprobrium if they champion certain strategies or challenge economic orthodoxy. Some entire sectors remain toxic, seemingly unable to reverse public sentiment about past bad behaviour. That is why you will find no bankers in *2020 Vision*. There is no one from the fast-food sector, from the defence industries, pharmaceuticals, nuclear energy or the chemicals sector. In these sectors, business leaders do not feel victimised by the charges against them. Rather, they feel misunderstood. The risk to their reputation outweighs the benefits from articulating their vision. Their unease is further compounded by a fear of contamination. When a company in a particular sector suffers a crisis, the reputational fall-out can infect the entire industry. All oil exploration companies were damaged by the Deepwater Horizon disaster that befell BP. All investment banks suffered from the collapse of Lehman Brothers. The reputation of retail banks has yet to recover from the sub-prime mortgage crisis. Pharmaceutical companies were hurt by the corruption charges levelled against GSK in China. Multiple companies face charges of moral failings in relation to legally legitimate strategies to minimise their tax exposure. All business fears for its reputation in this febrile environment.

What distinguishes the executives contributing to *2020 Vision* is a sense of positive change. They all lead companies that are, one way or another, useful indicators of wider economic activity. And most of them represent sectors that have escaped public controversy. Unlike their counterparts in banking or fast-food, for example, they proved willing to articulate the stories behind their current strategies and their plans for the future. But they all also recognise that delivering rising profits, generating cash and improving top-line revenues is no longer enough to secure public approval. Instead, the company chairmen, chief executives and board directors interviewed for this book increasingly feel the need to demonstrate a broader purpose. They have a society story to tell. Their overriding message is that companies must take advantage of structural change in different industries so that they can out-perform their rivals, enhance top-line revenues and exceed investor and consumer expectations. But they must do so while making a wider impact that leads to rising living standards, improved sustainability and better outcomes for individuals in every part of the value chain.

The visions expressed in this book come from twenty different industries, each shaped by differing economic and market trends. But the executives share a common sentiment: that business is undergoing a major transformation, driven by new technologies, globalisation, intense competition, pricing pressure, mounting regulation, growing environmental concerns and rapidly-changing consumer behaviour. The different strategies also sit against a backdrop of excess capacity, rising energy costs and volatile consumer confidence. That backdrop is forcing companies in multiple sectors to re-engineer their operations.

The engineering work portrayed in *2020 Vision* is not defensive, however. The company bosses in this book prefer to extol their strategic offensives. They are changing the way they do business to secure competitive advantage. They are collectively determined to innovate faster than their rivals. Yet none of the executives who agreed to be interviewed claims absolute success. There are no alchemists to be found in these pages. There is little room for complacency. But there is room for broad agreement on the economic, technical and geo-political trends that are reshaping industry.

Every business leader in this book agrees that companies of all shapes and sizes must address the challenges posed by the mega-trends of urbanisation, a digitised society, ageing populations and the need to serve the connected generation. These macro forces are coinciding with shifts in geographic power. The mature markets of North America, Western Europe and Japan remain vital engines of consumer demand and economic activity. But serving those markets requires different disciplines from those needed for the rapid-growth opportunities in China, India and the emerging economic powers such as Nigeria, Turkey, Indonesia and potentially Iran.

A common conclusion, articulated in several chapters, is that success in both mature and newer markets depends crucially on securing and retaining executive talent. Companies seem to be engaged in an arms race for the brightest and best scientists, the smartest researchers, innovative production managers, exceptional salespeople, outstanding client-handlers and the sort of digital experts who can deliver a competitive edge. Executive mobility, industrial expertise and digital fluency are in short supply in every industry. Put simply, demand is exceeding supply in the war for talent.

The other major requirement, shining through *2020 Vision*, is the need to harness the potential of big data. The four 'Vs' of big data – the growing volume, velocity, variety and veracity of digital information – are seen as both an opportunity and a threat. Business leaders know they must enhance their data capabilities, and that such data could unlock new ways to improve operating efficiency and reach new consumers. But they are concerned about how best to harness the ever-increasing volume of data, how to deal with the speed at which it is changing, how to calculate the cost-benefits of investing in data, and the regulatory implications behind gathering such information.

The businesses featured in these pages are all experimenting with data, while remaining unsure of the payback or about its practical application. Trial projects in this area and other aspects of digital technology may cause the 2010–20 decade to be remembered, commercially, as the age of experimentation. Executives are piloting new ways of delivering their business. They talk of greater consumer intimacy. They hope to penetrate new markets and to create products or services that will make their businesses, in whatever sector, the preferred choice for end customers. But they are not certain it will deliver success.

The pace of change will accelerate, driven primarily by technology. In 2015, the US Federal Trade Commission estimated that there will be more than 25 billion connected devices in circulation, from smartphones to wearable gadgets, all of which will share increasing amounts of information and computing power. This connectivity will expand exponentially as all forms of commerce adapt to the 'internet of things', where machine-to-machine communications replace human interaction online. Not enough companies are ready for this transition. Pilot projects are underway but they seem to be confined to sectors where R&D investment has always been a priority and where companies are anxious not to be left behind by Silicon Valley.

The sense of anxiety relates to the seemingly relentless ambition of US technology companies, many of which are diversifying from their core competence in social media with innovations in other sectors, notably automotives and aerospace. Clearly, companies such as Google are not about to become manufacturing rivals to GM or Boeing. But they are building proprietary software and artificial intelligence capabilities that could make them powerful suppliers to a range of industrial sectors. Given the spending power of Silicon Valley companies – with Apple becoming the most valuable company in the world by market capitalisation – executives in every sector should be wary of their existing business models being shaken up. Such innovations should deliver consumer benefits (at least for digitally literate consumers) but the benefits are less clear for employment, for investment and for shareholder returns.

What this means is that there is even less room for under-performance. Companies that fail to invest in technology or harness new market opportunities are likely to be swallowed up, face shareholder disquiet or at least change their management. The years from 2015 to 2020 will be a period of significant commercial disruption. No business is safe from the forces of technical change, additional regulation, new competitive pressures and increasingly demanding consumer expectations.

This uncertain horizon has become visible at a time of margin pressure and the need for companies to widen their geographic presence at a minimal cost of capital. It is happening at a time of growing environmental awareness. It is a period in which demands are rising for improved corporate governance, for greater diversity in decision making and for reinvestment in product development and job creation. This is the ultimate commercial challenge of the period to 2020. Success or failure will not be determined in short-term earnings cycles. The contributors to *2020 Vision* believe it will depend on structural change and relentless operational excellence.

Given that prescription, the participating chairmen, chief executives and directors might be forgiven for a shared sense of unease, if not outright pessimism. Yet for the most part they are optimists. These business leaders have a common survival instinct. They expect their companies to endure for the long term because of smart investment planning and product innovation, married to the opportunities created by new technology and globalisation.

For some of the contributors, this survival instinct reflects long-term familial ties. The chairmen and chief executives of family companies – Emma Marcegaglia, Jacob Wallenberg, Lord Rothermere, Ashish Thakkar and Enrique Zambrano – have a shared sense of guardianship. They are operating their businesses to ensure they can be passed on to the next generation of family ownership.

The sense of guardianship is not confined to family companies. It is also true of the large listed companies. Whether it is Sir Martin Sorrell of WPP, Jac Nasser at BHP Billiton or Linda Zecher at Houghton Mifflin Harcourt, they each hint at guardianship obligations towards employees, suppliers, shareholders and customers. If they cannot meet or safeguard the expectations of each of these groups, then no amount of visionary promises will make a difference.

This reality check exposes another common trait in this book: corporate pragmatism. None of the business leaders featured here are messianic about their visions. They tend to shun elaborate slogans or wordy mission statements. Instead, they talk of preserving goods and services that meet or, preferably, exceed consumer demand. Some believe they are engaged in enhancing living standards. Others say they are improving the means by which consumers communicate, travel or access services. Some are passionate about safety, learning skills or healthcare technology. All advocate rising international trade, more efficient sources of energy, lower costs of capital and the need to exploit digital technologies.

Those aspirations require companies to function effectively. Success depends on businesses becoming more efficient at what they already do, aided by minimal red-tape, properly-applied regulations, reduced protectionism and talented staff. Turning that vision into reality is far from certain. It risks being compromised by a worrying shortage of relevant and internationally mobile skills. Too many companies are not able to pivot from one course of action to another in pursuit of their ultimate goal – a strategy pursued aggressively at GE. And many business leaders lament the apparent triumph of austerity-minded procurement directors over costly product development, breakthrough research and long-term strategic planning. All this is compounded in some parts of the world, especially sub-Saharan Africa, by a shortage of infrastructural investment in the countries that need it most.

One thing is clear: without the services delivered by the companies in *2020 Vision*, the world would be a poorer place. Without digital learning, the education gap between differing economies is likely to widen. Without advances in medical technology, the problems caused by poor nutrition, diabetes and obesity will become even more challenging. Without advances in next-generation fuels for cars, ships and planes, the cost of transport and travel will escalate, and with it the cost of trade. Natural resources need to be extracted at lower cost, more safely and with reduced impact on the environment. Digital technology needs to be understood and distributed and used in a more practical and intuitive way. This must be achieved while delivering a solid return on investment and legitimate rewards for employees and shareholders. And it must be done in such a way that inspires consumer confidence.

This is what lies behind the visions set out in this book. Although each business faces its own challenges, there is more that unites than divides them. The companies contributing to *2020 Vision* have common anxieties. Their leaders offer similar diagnoses regarding what needs to be fixed. Where companies are vulnerable, care plans have been prepared to restore them to health. The visions are not grandiose or far beyond the horizon. They are relatively clear-sighted about what needs to be fixed. They must invest more in new technology; they must adapt more rapidly to changing consumer trends; and they must redefine themselves as part of the solution to the major challenges posed by urbanisation, climate change, ageing populations, and a more discerning and connected generation of customers.

Every business leader wants their company to excel and innovate at what it does best. The trouble is, none knows exactly how fast their accepted way of doing business could be turned on its head. So even the most optimistic business leader has a nagging sense of vulnerability about the future. For investors and consumers, that may be a good thing. It concentrates corporate minds on innovation and relentless change. It means that the current generation of business leaders are more willing to take calculated risks in order to avoid failure. They have to combine existing operational excellence with opportunistic readiness to adapt, which in terms of business vision, demands huge dexterity. Any business leader who thinks their job is finished will be right about one thing only. They themselves will be finished.

INDEX